New Directions for Adult and Continuing Education

Susan Imel
Jovita M. Ross-Gordon
COEDITORS-IN-CHIEF

Bringing Community to the Adult ESL Classroom

Clarena Larrotta
Ann K. Brooks
EDITORS

Number 121 • Spring 2009
Jossey-Bass
San Francisco

Bringing Community to the Adult ESL Classroom
Clarena Larrotta, Ann K. Brooks (eds)
New Directions for Adult and Continuing Education, no. 121
Susan Imel, Jovita M. Ross-Gordon, Coeditors-in-Chief

Microfilm copies of issues and articles are available in 16mm and 35mm, as well as microfiche in 105mm, through University Microfilms Inc., 300 North Zeeb Road, Ann Arbor, Michigan 48106-1346.

New Directions for Adult and Continuing Education (ISSN 1052-2891, electronic ISSN 1536-0717) is part of The Jossey-Bass Higher and Adult Education Series and is published quarterly by Wiley Subscription Services, Inc., A Wiley Company, at Jossey-Bass, 989 Market Street, San Francisco, California 94103-1741. Periodicals Postage Paid at San Francisco, California, and at additional mailing offices. POSTMASTER: Send address changes to New Directions for Adult and Continuing Education, Jossey-Bass, 989 Market Street, San Francisco, California 94103-1741.

New Directions for Adult and Continuing Education is indexed in CIJE: Current Index to Journals in Education (ERIC); Contents Pages in Education (T&F); ERIC Database (Education Resources Information Center; Higher Education Abstracts (Claremont Graduate University); and Sociological Abstracts (CSA/CIG).

Subscriptions cost $89.00 for individuals and $228.00 for institutions, agencies, and libraries.

Editorial correspondence should be sent to the Coeditors-in-Chief, Susan Imel, ERIC/ACVE, 1900 Kenny Road, Columbus, Ohio 43210-1090, e-mail: imel.l@osu.edu; or Jovita M. Ross-Gordon, Southwest Texas State University, EAPS Dept., 601 University Drive, San Marcos, TX 78666.

Cover photograph by Jack Hollingsworth@Photodisc

www.josseybass.com

CONTENTS

EDITORS' NOTES   1
Clarena Larrotta, Ann K. Brooks

1.   Assessing the Literacy Skills of Adult Immigrants and Adult   5
English Language Learners
Heide Spruck Wrigley, Jing Chen, Sheida White, and Jaleh Soroui
This chapter addresses implications of findings from the 2007 National
Assessment of Adult Literacy (NAAL) survey. It reports on social and
employment issues affecting foreign-born and U.S.-born adults who are
not yet proficient in English and the implications for program planning
and implementation of adult ESOL programs and services.

2.   Best Practices for Teaching the "Whole" Adult ESL Learner   25
David Schwarzer
An adult ESL educator provides useful guidelines for novice-adult ESL
instructors. He presents "whole language principles" as a way to build
community in the adult ESL classroom.

3.   Journaling in an Adult ESL Literacy Program   35
Clarena Larrotta
This chapter demonstrates how dialogue journal writing can provide
different opportunities for community building and for English literacy
development to happen.

4.   Identity Issues in Building an ESL Community: The Puerto   45
Rican Experience
Betsy Morales, Eileen K. Blau
Two adult ESL instructors share their experiences teaching in a bilingual
community in the Caribbean. They explore sociocultural and identity
issues as they impact the ESL classroom.

5.   Community in a Hurry: Social Contracts and Social   55
Covenants in Short-Term ESL Courses
Rob A. Martinsen
A language instructor discusses the difficulties building community in
short-term English language courses. He provides useful suggestions for
implementing social contracts and social covenants with adult ESL
students on the bases of trust.

6. Complexity and Community: Finding What Works   65
in Workplace ESL

Ann K. Brooks
This chapter presents best practices in helping ELL's function in the
workplace within the context of three communities of practice: Adult
ESL education, training and development, and human resource
management.

7. Final Thoughts on Community in Adult ESL   75

Clarena Larrotta
This chapter briefly discusses emergent themes from the various
contributions to this volume as well as implications for adult ESL
education practice.

INDEX   79

EDITORS' NOTES

Contributions to This Volume

The contributors to this volume come from different institutions and have worked or are currently working in different adult ESL learning contexts. They explore the ways in which classroom community can be built and ESL learning and learners can be integrated in the broader civic and workplace communities. They address the different contexts of ESL learning and teaching. The chapters in this volume present the authors' professional and research experiences and make important connections between theory and practice. More importantly, the authors share their points of view inviting graduate students, language instructors, adult educators, and researchers to analyze their own beliefs and practices regarding adult learning, and adult ESL education and research.

Heide Spruck Wrigley, Jing Chen, Sheida White, and Jaleh Soroui contribute the first chapter in the volume. This chapter uses data from the 2007 NAAL, National Assessment of Adult Literacy, (National Center for Educational Statistics), to describe the socio-economic and language characteristics of foreign-born and U.S.-born English language learning adults in the U.S. Their analysis has crucial implications for the future provision and funding of services for both immigrants and U.S.-born adults with literacy needs. Their chapter is set against the current pressure in the U.S. to raise the general level of education among all adults of all language backgrounds.

In the following chapters, David Schwarzer, Clarena Larrotta, and Rob Martinsen describe the role an instructor can play in building community in the classroom and integrating ESL instruction into the broader communities in which ESL learners live and work. David Schwarzer describes how second language acquisition theory can be implemented through using whole language philosophy with adult language learners. The focus of his chapter is on ESL community programs and the characteristics of volunteer instructors serving in those programs and provides suggestions for teaching ESL to adults in this context.

Clarena Larrotta shares her experiences implementing journaling in a non-profit adult ESL literacy program with Hispanic adults. Her chapter illustrates the roles both the ESL instructor and the adult learners play in enabling a classroom community to form. More than just explaining how to implement dialogue journals with adult ESL learners, she shares her students' comments and examples of their work, putting her students at the

NEW DIRECTIONS FOR ADULT AND CONTINUING EDUCATION, no. 121, Spring 2009 © 2009 Wiley Periodicals, Inc.
Published online in Wiley InterScience (www.interscience.wiley.com) • DOI: 10.1002/ace.320

1

center of this learning experience. She also emphasizes the importance of using a dialogic approach to writing and communicating in ESL.

Rob Martinsen reflects on the intricacies of community-building in short-term courses and draws on data he collected while teaching a six-week ESL course to adult learners. He presents a realistic picture of what it means for an instructor to earn his students' trust and to help them create a community of learners. He explains how to implement social contracts and social covenants with adult ESL students and describes how learner stakes in their civic community brings deep meaning to their language learning.

Betsy Morales, a bilingual Puerto Rican-American, and Eileen K. Blau, a New Yorker and Puerto Rican at heart, explore some of the identity issues influencing the teaching and learning of English in adult ESL classrooms in Puerto Rico. They examine how identity and culture influence English language learning in a community where the students are exposed to English outside the classroom, but feel that their own culture and native language (Spanish) are at risk of being overtaken by the U.S. language and culture.

Finally, in her chapter on workplace ESL, Ann K. Brooks explores what three different communities of practice see as best practices for providing immigrants with the language and opportunities they need to become contributing members of their workplace communities. She looks at adult ESL education, training and development, and human resource management and examines the interests and values of each. She then identifies both the patterns among and the unique contributions of each community of practice to the challenges of workplace language-learning and the integration of immigrants into workplace communities.

Clarena Larrotta
Editor

Theoretical Perspective

Due to the increasing number of adult English language learners (ELLs), adult educator practitioners and researchers have increasingly focused attention on the teaching and learning of English as a second language (ESL). This volume, *Bringing Community to the Adult ESL Classroom*, grows out of our experiences working with adult ELLs. It also grows out of changes in the field of second language acquisition, which suggest that adult language learning and teaching are most effective when they occur within the context of a "community."

Following general trends in learning theory and teaching practice over the last twenty years, second language acquisition has seen a "sociocultural" turn in how it understands language learning (Zuengler and Miller, 2006; Tarone, 2007; Johnson, 2006; Firth and Wagner, 1997). This has been a turn away from a singular focus on the language itself to a focus that includes the social context and human interactions that produce the language.

This turn has meant that many in the field now see language as a social tool that shapes the processes of the mind rather than as a system of symbols that is separate from its users (Vygotsky, 1978). Thus, language teachers do not solely focus on the "nuts and bolts" of the language (sentence structure, pronunciation, grammar) with the idea that students will take the language they have learned into the world and apply it. Instead it requires us to bring the social world into our classrooms, teaching learners the nuts and bolts within the context of authentic social interactions. It means we must understand that as our students are learning a language, they are also changing aspects of themselves and how they understand the world.

This turn has also meant that many in the field have shifted from viewing language learners as "consumers" to viewing them as "producers" of their new language as they participate in dialogue both within and outside of the classroom (Bakhtin, 1982). This has given new power to language learners to bring their own knowledge, experiences, and cultures to English, and as they dialogue with others, contribute to the ongoing process of developing and changing the language. For teachers, this means that our classrooms become places of creativity, where all participants bring what resources they possess to the ongoing dialogic interaction of social sharing, new knowledge creation, and language learning. This acknowledges that ESL speakers, as they have for generations in this country, bring new vocabulary from other languages to English and enrich U.S. cultures with the best and the most interesting of the cultures they bring with them.

Finally, the sociolinguistic turn has given new legitimacy to the knowledge language teachers have gained through their own learning and teaching practices and through their ability to continually build and refine their practice and theories of language learning and teaching in a rich praxis of reflection and action. It has placed cognitively-oriented psycholinguistic theory and related linguistic descriptions of English in the position of being a resource to be used by language teachers, but not the major focus of our teaching. Like linguists then, teachers, too, become creators of knowledge, observing and reflecting on what goes on in their classes, looking to theory for new (although not necessarily "right") perspectives on what is occurring in their classes and their own practice.

Although changes in second language acquisition might be enough of a reason for this volume, we were also motivated by the deep belief that ESL teachers have both the privilege and responsibility to help new immigrants integrate into our cities, neighborhoods, and organizations. The U.S. has a heritage of individualism, alien to many immigrants, and recent social trends such as two-career families, suburban sprawl, generational changes in values, and the substitution of experts and institutions for human relationships have exacerbated the isolation that many feel (Block, 2008; Putnam, 2001; Bellah, Madsen, Sullivan, Swidler, and Tipton, 1985). While many who were born here feel isolation and loneliness, immigrants may be even more vulnerable to these feelings.

ESL teachers can help to transform the experience of immigrants to this country by using activities in our classes that value relatedness.

Relatedness grows in a learning context that enables learners to share and have conversations about what they know, can do, care about, worry about, and hope for. It grows in a context where people listen and pay attention to each other. Relatedness flourishes within the context of community, and community is created "one room at a time" (Block, 2008). In the small group of an ESL classroom, as we learn the ways in which each of us is human, we build bridges not only between class members, but between nations and cultures, as well.

Migration worldwide has more than doubled in the last twenty-five years. Of the 190,633,564 migrants in 2005, 13,471,181 were refugees (Population Division of the Department of Economic and Social Affairs of the United Nations Secretariat, 2005). Many of those in the current diaspora are unable to return to their homelands. ESL teachers have the privilege and the opportunity to foster belonging and safety for our students and in this way to work to create and nurture communities that span the world.

References

Bakhtin, M. *The Dialogic Imagination: Four Essays*. Translated by K. Bostrom. Edited by M. Holquist and V. Liapunov, University of Texas Slavic Series. Austin: University of Texas Press, 1982.

Bellah, R. N., Madsen, R., Sullivan, W. M., Swidler, A., and Tipton, S. M. *Habits of the Heart: Individualism and Commitment in American Life*. Berkeley, CA: University of California Press, 1985.

Block, P. *Community: The Structure of Belonging*. San Francisco: Berrett-Koehler, 2008.

Firth, A. and Wagner, J. "On Discourse, Communication, and (Some) Fundamental Concepts of SLA Research." The Modern Language Journal, 1997, *81*(3), 285–300.

Johnson, K. E. "The Sociocultural Turn and Its Challenges for Second Language Teacher Education." TESOL Quarterly, 2006, *40*(1), 235–257.

National Center for Educational Statistics. National Assessment of Adult Literacy (NAAL). http://nces.ed.gov/naal/.

Putnam, R. D. Bowling Alone: The Collapse and Revival of American Community. New York: Simon and Schuster, 2001.

Tarone, E. "Sociolinguistic Approaches to Second Language Acquisition Research – 1997–2007." 2007, *91*(Focus Issue), 837–848.

Population Division of the Department of Economic and Social Affairs of the United Nations Secretariat. Trends in Total Migrant Stock: The 2005 Revision. Retrieved Sunday, August 03, 2008, from http://esa.un.org/migration.

Vygotsky, L. Mind in Society: The Development of Higher Psychological Processes. Cambridge, MA: Harvard University Press, 1978.

Zuengler, J., and Miller, E. R. "Cognitive and Sociocultural Perspectives: Two Parallel SLA Worlds?" *2006 TESOL Quarterly*, *40*(1), 35–58.

Ann K. Brooks
Editor

CLARENA LARROTTA is assistant professor at Texas State University–San Marcos. She teaches in the Adult, Professional, and Community Education Program.

ANN K. BROOKS is a professor of adult education at Texas State University–San Marcos.

New Directions for Adult and Continuing Education • DOI: 10.1002/ace

This chapter examines the characteristics and performance of adult immigrants and adult English language learners on the National Assessment of Adult Literacy. These factors are related to key social outcomes such as involvement in the labor force, income, and welfare participation, and the data reported can be used in making decisions about program planning, as well as in implementation of adult ESOL programs and services.

Assessing the Literacy Skills of Adult Immigrants and Adult English Language Learners

Heide Spruck Wrigley, Jing Chen, Sheida White, Jaleh Soroui

Most adults who are new to English manage to find work, raise children, and act as informed community members and citizens (Castro and Wiley, 2008). However, proficiency in English, particularly the ability to read and write the kind of English that educated adults use, goes hand in hand with access to a much broader range of information and affords a wider set of opportunities, particularly economic opportunities. Millions of the foreign-born come to the United States to find work and are a substantial and growing segment of the workforce. However, most immigrants are concentrated in entry-level low-wage jobs that cannot sustain a family (Wrigley and Powrie, 2008), and many end up working two or three minimum-wage jobs.

English proficiency is an important factor affecting wages and opportunities. Some studies (Martinez and Wang, 2006) report a 46 percent wage differential between immigrants who speak English and those who do not, even after adjusting for education and work experience. Other recent studies make it clear that English proficiency and level of education function together. One analysis, for example, showed that the mean annual earnings of immigrant workers with no more than a high school education rose steadily with their self-reported level of English-speaking skill (Sum, 2007).

NEW DIRECTIONS FOR ADULT AND CONTINUING EDUCATION, no. 121, Spring 2009 © 2009 Wiley Periodicals, Inc.
Published online in Wiley InterScience (www.interscience.wiley.com) • DOI: 10.1002/ace.321

While English matters, level of education matters as well. As other analyses have shown, English fluency along with twelve years of education can result in a 76 percent increase in earnings. However, there is only a 4 percent rise in income for those who are fluent in English but have fewer than eight years of education (Fermstad, 2003).

The negative effects of limited English increase with the level of education and work experience of immigrant workers (Sum, 2007), and limited English skills have a greater negative impact on immigrants with more education. Both the United States and Canada are finding that highly educated immigrants with limited English proficiency are much less likely than others who have better English skills to obtain technical, managerial, or professional jobs similar to those they held in their native countries (Comings, Sum, and Uvin, 2001).

For those wanting to improve their English language and literacy skills, the U.S. system provides free (or nearly free) classes for adults not yet proficient in English. However, in some areas such as New York, demand outstrips supply, and applicants are put on a waiting list. In spite of the general availability of courses in most areas of the country, only 45 percent of immigrants report participating in or having participated in adult English as a second language (ESL) classes.

Many reasons exist for not participating, including long waiting lists in many areas of the country and difficulties in getting to classes. Personal factors such as insufficient time due to family and work obligations, lack of dependable child care, and turbulence in one's life also affect participation. In addition, the life skills focus that predominates in most of the adult ESL classes for immigrants may not match the interests of adults, who feel they have sufficient survival skills to cope in a new environment and are looking for programs that are either more academically oriented (to facilitate transition to Adult Basic Education classes or community college) or offer the language needed for job skills training (Wrigley, 2007).

Despite growing awareness of both the need and the demand for English language and literacy programs, not much is known about the specific language skill levels of adult immigrants and adult English language learners (ELLs). The Census Bureau provides information on immigrants' educational backgrounds and how well foreign-born adults speak and understand English (oral proficiency), but it provides no data on their ability to comprehend or use print and make sense of written documents, such as newspapers, announcements, or job descriptions.

Analysis by the National Assessment of Adult Literacy (NAAL; National Center for Education Statistics, 2003) links level of literacy to the social and employment needs of those who are not yet proficient in English, be they foreign-born or U.S.-born adults. In particular, it provides guidance on services for the most vulnerable group of immigrants, those who are new to English and have few years of education. It includes a discussion of both foreign-born and U.S.-born ELLs.

In light of changing demographics and the increasing U.S. reliance on immigrant labor, and given the negative impact of limited English proficiency on the acquisition and full utilization of existing skills and education in work, an urgent need exists for a nuanced picture of the skill levels and skill gaps of different groups of immigrants and ELLs. The data and insights presented here provide a basis for identifying these language and literacy needs so that they can be addressed.

Defining Limited English Proficiency

Government agencies define ELLs who are still of limited English proficiency (LEP) as individuals "who were not born in the United States or whose language is a language other than English and whose difficulties in speaking, reading, writing or understanding the English language may deny the individual the opportunity to participate fully in society" (U.S. Department of Education, 2002).

Types of Proficiency. Linguists studying second-language acquisition distinguish among at least three types of proficiency:

1. *Full proficiency in English,* meaning a second-language speaker is competent in all skill areas—reading, writing, speaking, and listening—although some influence from the native language is likely to be present
2. *Oral proficiency,* meaning the person is competent when speaking English and has few difficulties understanding what other English speakers are saying
3. *Written proficiency,* or the ability to understand and use print to make meaning

Only written proficiency (the competence required to negotiate print) is measured by the NAAL, although the assessment also includes self-reports on oral proficiency.

Definitions Used in Reporting NAAL Findings. Our analysis of the NAAL is organized around two key categories: immigrants and English language learners.

• Immigrants are adults who were born in a foreign country, including U.S. territories and other foreign countries. Immigrants may be English-speaking or non-English-speaking.

• English language learners are adults who learned to speak a language other than English before starting school. They may be foreign-born or U.S.-born. Our analysis further subdivides ELLs into Spanish speakers (the majority of ELLs) and non-Spanish speakers (everyone else).

Figure 1.1 shows how adults assessed by the NAAL can be subcategorized into foreign-born and U.S.-born adults on the one hand and into English language learners and non–English language learners on the other.

New Directions for Adult and Continuing Education • DOI: 10.1002/ace

Figure 1.1. Categories and Subcategories of NAAL Participants

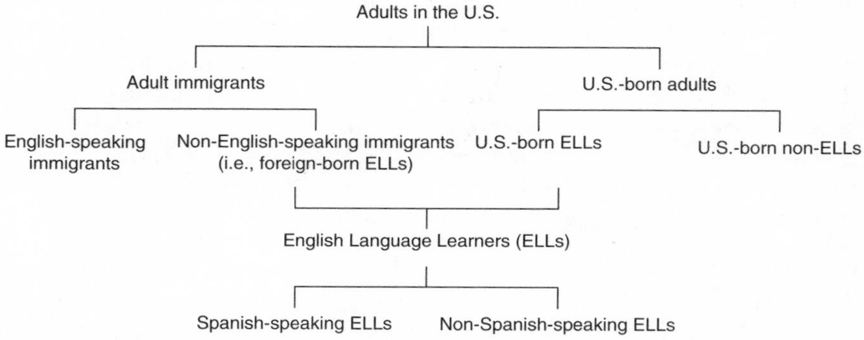

```
                          Adults in the U.S.
            ┌──────────────────────┴──────────────────────┐
     Adult immigrants                              U.S.-born adults
   ┌────────┴──────────┐                     ┌───────────┴───────────┐
English-speaking  Non-English-speaking immigrants  U.S.-born ELLs   U.S.-born non-ELLs
immigrants        (i.e., foreign-born ELLs)
                           └───────────┬───────────┘
                          English Language Learners (ELLs)
                           ┌───────────┴───────────┐
                  Spanish-speaking ELLs    Non-Spanish-speaking ELLs
```

Data Source

The data in this chapter come from the 2003 National Assessment of Adult Literacy conducted by the National Center for Education Statistics (NCES) of the U.S. Department of Education's Institute of Education Sciences. The NAAL examines the literacy skills of a wide range of adults and includes both native speakers of English and English language learners. ELLs are made up of two groups: (1) adults who are foreign-born and (2) adults who were born in the United States but who spoke a language other than English before starting school. The NAAL participants are nationally representative of adults aged sixteen and older residing in households or prisons in the United States (Kutner, Greenberg, Jin, and Paulson, 2006).

The assessment measures the ability to perform literacy tasks similar to those encountered in daily life. The NAAL literacy tasks examine prose literacy (to search, comprehend, and use continuous texts, such as a consent form), document literacy (to search, comprehend, and use noncontinous texts such as job applications), and quantitative literacy (to identify and perform computation, such as calculating a tip). This chapter will focuses mostly on prose literacy, which we also refer to as English literacy. The results for document and quantitative literacy are similar.

The interviewers administered the assessment in person, one on one, in participants' homes or in a classroom or library in the prison from March 2003 through January 2004. After assuring selected individuals that their responses would be confidential and the scores would only be reported in aggregate, interviewers administered the background questionnaire to those who chose to participate using a computer-assisted personal interviewing system programmed into laptop computers. The interviewers read the background questions from the computer screen and entered all responses directly into the computer. The background questionnaires were administered orally in either English or Spanish, whichever language the participant chose. The oral administration and the Spanish language option enabled more adults at the low end of the literacy continuum to understand and answer the questions about their backgrounds.

Upon completion of the background questionnaires, researchers handed participants booklets containing assessment tasks. Each assessment booklet began with the same seven easy tasks. Based on the performance of the seven tasks, interviewers used an algorithm to determine whether the participants should continue in the main assessment or be placed in the Adult Literacy Supplemental Assessment (ALSA). ALSA offers an easier set of literacy tasks designed specifically for adults who have very limited English literacy skills (White and Dillow, 2005).

To facilitate meaningful reporting of adult performance, the NAAL groups literacy scores into four performance levels—below-basic, basic, intermediate, and proficient (White and Dillow, 2005; Hauser, Edley, Koenig, and Elliot, 2005). Those given the ALSA had incorrectly answered most or all of the seven easiest tasks at the beginning of the main NAAL assessment and were classified at the below-basic level on all scales.

While such factors as educational attainment and length of time in the United States differ among the foreign-born populations, some characteristics predominate.

Ethnicity, Age, and Educational Attainment. Latinos make up 52 percent of the foreign-born population but only 6 percent of the native-born population. About half (55 percent) of the foreign-born but only 42 percent of the native-born are between the ages of sixteen and thirty. Only 8 percent of the foreign-born but 16 percent of the U.S.-born are sixty-five years of age or older. Most of the foreign-born (64 percent) immigrated at a relatively young age (at or before age twenty-four). Table 1.1 elaborates the distinctions between the foreign- and U.S.-born regarding race and ethnicity, age, and level of education.

Whereas the share of those who have completed only a few years of high school is more than twice as high among the foreign-born as the U.S.-born (32 percent versus 13 percent), the percentage of those who have at least one college degree is the same among both groups (23 percent and 22 percent, respectively). Although a significant number of immigrants have college degrees, the educational levels of the foreign-born population overall are significantly lower than those of the U.S.-born. A smaller percentage of foreign-born than native-born adults have a GED or some other form of high school completion (20 percent versus 33 percent) and an even smaller percentage have some college, an associate's degree, or some other two-year degree (16 percent versus 24 percent). At the lower levels of education, over half (52 percent) of the foreign-born, compared to 46 percent of U.S.-born adults, have no more than a high school education.

This wide range of educational backgrounds in the foreign-born population has strong implications for educational services. The relative youth of immigrants speaks to the need for transition programs for out-of-school youth and young adults that not only focus on language and literacy development but also make access to academic and occupational opportunities easier.

New Directions for Adult and Continuing Education • DOI: 10.1002/ace

Table 1.1. Distribution of Foreign-Born and U.S.-Born Adults, by Selected Characteristics

Characteristic	Foreign-born	U.S.-born
Race/Ethnicity		
White	21	79
Black	9	12
Hispanic	52	6
Asian/Pacific Islander	18	1
Other	1	3
Age		
16–18	4	6
19–24	12	10
25–39	39	26
40–49	20	20
50–64	16	22
65+	8	16
Educational attainment		
Still in high school	4	3
Less than/some high school	32	13
GED/high school graduate	20	33
Vocational/trade/business school	6	5
Some college	7	12
Associate's/2-year degree	9	12
College degree or above	23	22

Source: U.S. Department of Education, National Center for Education Statistics. *National Assessment of Adult Literacy (NAAL)*. Washington, D.C.: Government Printing Office, 2003.

Employment, Income, and Welfare Participation. The employment picture for immigrants is not significantly different from that for native-born adults (see Table 1.2). Slightly more than half are employed full time (57 percent of immigrants, 52 percent of native-born). About a quarter of both groups are not in the labor force and not looking for work, and about 8 percent are unemployed and looking for work.

Although immigrants have employment rates on a par with those of native-born adults, they are generally poorer. Almost 30 percent of the foreign-born, compared to 16 percent of U.S.-born adults, report household income below the poverty threshold. About half of all immigrants (49 percent) are "nonpoor" or have a family income that exceeds 175 percent of the poverty level (67 percent of native-born adults are nonpoor). The extent to which immigrants are poor or nonpoor differs by ethnicity. Sixty-one percent of Spanish speakers, compared to 39 percent of non–Spanish speakers, had incomes below the poverty line. These numbers point to the importance of creating educational and occupational opportunities designed for Spanish speakers to help provide access to family sustaining employment.

New Directions for Adult and Continuing Education • DOI: 10.1002/ace

Table 1.2. Distribution of Adult Immigrants and U.S.-Born Adults, by Employment Status, Household Income, and Welfare Participation

Characteristics	Adult immigrants	U.S.-born adults
Employment status		
Not in labor force	24	28
Unemployed, looking for work	8	8
Part-time	11	13
Full-time	57	52
Household income		
Below poverty threshold	29	16
100–125% above threshold	9	6
126–150% above threshold	7	5
151–175% above threshold	6	6
Above 175% of threshold	49	67
Welfare participation		
Never	94	93
Past participation	4	6
Current participation	2	1

Source: U.S. Department of Education, National Center for Education Statistics. *National Assessment of Adult Literacy (NAAL).* Washington, D.C.: Government Printing Office, 2003.

A common misperception is that rates of welfare participation by immigrants are higher than those for U.S.-born adults. The NAAL data do not support this. The vast majority of participants in the NAAL (94 percent) reported never having been on welfare, which is the same as for U.S.-born adults. This holds true for both Spanish speakers and other adult English language learners.

Comparing Foreign-Born and U.S.-Born English Language Learners

More than half of the foreign-born ELLs say their oral English skills are sound (see Table 1.3). About 60 percent report speaking English either "very well" (33 percent) or "well" (29 percent). That means that over half of immigrant ELLs are likely to have the conversational skills necessary to negotiate everyday tasks, find jobs, enroll their children in school, access basic services, and handle day-to-day activities that require English. Of those who reported speaking English less than well, about 15 percent said they spoke no English, and almost a quarter reported speaking English "not well." Although it is possible to acquire oral English skills through day-to-day exposure to the language, many of those who speak no English would be well served by ESL programs that stress the acquisition of oral communication skills along with English literacy. Those who are both new to English and new to the United

New Directions for Adult and Continuing Education • DOI: 10.1002/ace

Table 1.3. Distribution of Foreign-Born and U.S.-Born English Language Learners, by Self-Reported Oral English Proficiency, Educational Attainment, Employment Status, and Household Income

Characteristics	Foreign-born ELLs	U.S.-born ELLs
Self-reported oral English proficiency		
Very well	33	85
Well	29	13
Not well	25	2
Not at all	14	1
Educational attainment		
Still in high school	4	5
Less than/some high school	35	16
GED/high school graduate	20	32
Vocational/trade/business school	6	5
Some college	6	12
Associate's/2-year degree	8	13
College degree or above	21	18
Employment status		
Not in labor force	24	32
Unemployed, looking for work	7	10
Part-time	11	14
Full-time	57	45
Household income		
Below poverty threshold	31	23
100–125% above threshold	10	7
126–150% above threshold	7	8
151–175% above threshold	7	7
Above 175% of threshold	46	55

Source: U.S. Department of Education, National Center for Education Statistics. *National Assessment of Adult Literacy (NAAL).* Washington, D.C.: Government Printing Office, 2003.

States will benefit from programs that provide both English language and cultural orientation.

The data on U.S.-born ELLs or second-generation Americans who speak a language other than English before starting school are more positive than for foreign-born immigrants. Almost all U.S.-born ELLs (98 percent) consider themselves fairly proficient in English, with 85 percent saying they speak English "very well" and 13 percent reporting that they speak English "well." Clearly, these adults believe they possess what the linguistic literature calls basic interactive communication skills. They have the proficiency needed to interact with others in English in social situations, carry on conversations, and communicate their ideas successfully in face-to-face or phone conversations.

Differences in education between foreign-born and U.S.-born ELLs are also striking. The percentage of adults who have not completed high school

New Directions for Adult and Continuing Education • DOI: 10.1002/ace

is over twice as high for foreign-born (35 percent) as for U.S.-born ELLs (16 percent).

Although more foreign-born ELLs (57 percent) than U.S.-born ELLs (45 percent) are working full time, household incomes for the foreign-born are more limited than for the U.S.-born. Thirty-one percent of foreign-born versus 23 percent of all U.S. households report incomes below the poverty threshold, and only 46 percent of the foreign-born ELLs earn in excess of 175 percent of the poverty threshold, compared to 55 percent of their U.S.-born counterparts.

Comparing Spanish-Speaking ELLs and Speakers of Other Languages

Significant differences exist between Spanish- and non-Spanish-speaking ELLs regarding educational background and literacy abilities (see Table 1.4). Spanish speakers report fewer years of education and demonstrate lower English literacy skills. Nearly four times as many Spanish speakers (42 percents) as non-Spanish-speaking ELLs (11 percent) did not complete high school. Lack of high school completion continues to be a concern among Hispanic youth both for foreign-born teenagers, who may never have gone to school or whose schooling may have been interrupted, and for those who were born in the United States. The NAAL underscores the nature of that

Table 1.4. Educational Attainment Levels and Prose Literacy Performance Levels of English Language Learners, by Spanish-Speaking Status, 2003

Characteristics	Spanish-speaking ELLs	Non-Spanish-speaking ELLs
Total	55.5	44.5
Educational attainment		
Still in high school	6	2
Less than/some high school	42	11
GED/high school graduate	24	25
Vocational/trade/business school	5	6
Some college	7	9
Associate's/2-year degree	7	13
College degree or above	9	33
Prose		
Below Basic	50	18
Basic	28	34
Intermediate	19	40
Proficient	3	8

Source: U.S. Department of Education, National Center for Education Statistics. *National Assessment of Adult Literacy (NAAL).* Washington, D.C.: Government Printing Office, 2003.

need. These findings have strong implications for education and training. There is a clear need for models that not only increase the reading and writing skills of Spanish speakers but also fill the educational gaps related to math or science for those with few years of schooling experience.

We also see important differences in educational achievement at the higher end of the scale. Again, non–Spanish speakers have many more years of schooling than their Spanish-speaking counterparts; a full one-third of non–Spanish speakers, compared to only 9 percent of Spanish speakers, have at least a college degree. Given the relatively high educational levels of non–Spanish speakers, policymakers and program developers may want to consider the establishment of accelerated ESL classes for those whose background knowledge and experience with schooling allow them to progress faster than those who lack both academic knowledge and study skills. For those with professional degrees from other countries, programs and services that facilitate accreditation and certification (or reaccreditation and recertification) and focus on English for Special Purposes can help foreign-born professionals move into the workforce more quickly and allow the country to integrate their high-level skills into the workforce.

English Language Learners' Levels of English Literacy

As discussed earlier, the majority of English language learners speak English quite well. About three quarters of all ELLs report speaking English either "very well" (51 percent) or "well" (23 percent). Only 17 percent report speaking English "not well," and 9 percent report speaking English "not at all." However, literacy in English is another matter entirely, and only a small percentage (6 percent) of ELLs score in the proficient range of English literacy.

About two-thirds of English language learners scored either in the below-basic (35 percent) or basic (31 percent) category. Another 28 percent had scores in the intermediate range. These numbers highlight the strong difference between immigrants' oral proficiency in English and low English literacy skills. This mismatch points toward the need to put a greater emphasis on promoting reading and writing, especially for those language learners whose goal it is to continue their education and gain access to skilled or professional jobs.

Differences in English Literacy Levels. Not surprisingly, since education and literacy attainment often go hand in hand, the English literacy skills of Spanish speakers (most of whom have low levels of educational achievement) are not as strong as those of other groups. Half of all Spanish speakers scored in the below-basic category on prose literacy, while only 18 percent of non-Spanish-speaking ELLs scored this low. Similarly, only 22 percent of Spanish speakers, compared to almost 50 percent of non–Spanish speakers, scored in the intermediate or proficient range.

Comparing Literacy Levels of ELLs and Native Speakers of English. Literacy is a critical determinant of economic success, not just for people who spoke a language other than English growing up but for native speakers as

New Directions for Adult and Continuing Education • DOI: 10.1002/ace

Figure 1.2. Prose Literacy Levels of Adults, by English Language Learner Status, 2003

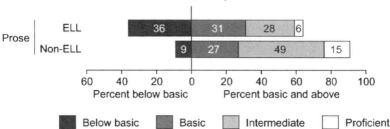

Source: U.S. Department of Education, National Center for Education Statistics. *National Assessment of Adult Literacy (NAAL)*. Washington, D.C.: Government Printing Office, 2003.

well. As can be expected, important differences appear between English learners and those who grew up speaking only English, although both groups had difficulty understanding more complex texts. Only 6 percent of ELLs scored proficient in prose, compared to about twice as many native speakers (see Figure 1.2). These results signal that both groups need to upgrade their skills in order to be competitive, although the road to full literacy is likely to be significantly longer and more arduous for English language learners. While native speakers come to print with oral fluency in English, ELLs face the dual challenge of having to develop their spoken language skills along with their print literacy skills.

A similar difference emerges at the bottom of the scale. Here the percentage of ELLs who can read only isolated words or phrases and recognize a few signs is four times as high as the percentage of native speakers at that level. Interestingly, there is much less of a difference between the two groups when it comes to basic literacy. Between a quarter and two-thirds of both groups could only read basic and below-basic texts and had trouble with more challenging texts.

Comparing ELLs with Below-Basic English Literacy Skills to Those Who Are Proficient. Policy reports have shown that recent arrivals to the United States have lower English skills than previous immigrants, which limits their ability to find work and earn enough to support their families (Wrigley and others, 2003; McHugh, Gelatt, and Fix, 2007). Many also lack the education and training credentials critical to advancement in the labor market.

Very low levels of literacy limit the opportunities of all adults, foreign- or U.S.-born, to engage in civic activities, such as voting or working with English-speaking neighbors to address community concerns. Those who scored below basic may be able to identify single words and phrases but have difficulty making sense of even simple connected texts, such as announcements or short descriptions. They are likely to fall into two categories: those who are relatively new to English and neither speak nor read much English and those who speak English adequately but have difficulties reading and writing in English. From a program-planning and policy perspective, those who score low but are relatively new to the United States are of less concern. We know that as overall English skills improve, English literacy is likely to improve as well, at least for those who have literacy skills in their native language.

Age and Newcomer Status. Over three-quarters of ELLs with below-basic English literacy (78 percent) were Spanish speakers. Non–Spanish speakers who scored below basic were older than their Spanish-speaking counterparts. More than half of non-Spanish-speaking ELLs were over fifty, and half of that group was over sixty-five years old, whereas only 10 percent of Spanish speakers were over sixty-five. These older adults may have been refugees who had never held a pencil or immigrants who lived in areas in the United States where English literacy is not necessary to live and function. Important to remember is that older adults who are not in the workforce may be able to function quite well without English literacy (Macias, 1994; Rivera, 2008; Castro and Wiley, 2008).

Most of the adults with very limited English literacy (63 percent) came to the United States as adults aged nineteen or older, and a good percentage of those were relative newcomers (see Table 1.5). Almost 30 percent of the

Table 1.5. Distribution of English Language Learners, Spanish-Speaking ELLs, and Non-Spanish-Speaking ELLs Who Scored Below-Basic in Prose Literacy, by Years Living in the United States and Age of Immigration

Years living in the United States	All ELLs scoring Below Basic in prose	Spanish-speaking ELLs scoring Below Basic in prose	Non-Spanish-speaking ELLs scoring Below Basic in prose
U.S. born	10	9	16
1–5 years	27	29	20
6–10 years	17	18	13
11–15 years	13	14	10
16–20 years	9	9	9
21–30 years	12	11	15
31 + years	12	11	17
Age of immigration			
U.S. born	10	9	16
11	5	6	4
12 to 18	22	24	14
19 to 24	26	26	24
25 +	37	35	42

Source: U.S. Department of Education, National Center for Education Statistics. *National Assessment of Adult Literacy (NAAL).* Washington, D.C.: Government Printing Office, 2003.

Spanish speakers and 20 percent of the non–Spanish speakers had been in the country for less than six years. When we look at the remaining new-comers, we see that the non–Spanish speakers tend to be much more estab-lished. About 32 percent had been in the United States for over twenty years, and among those, about 17 percent had been in the country for thirty-one years or more.

Educational Attainment. The vast majority of ELLs who scored below basic had either not completed high school (63 percent) or had only a high school education (22 percent). A few, on the other hand, had a solid education but were barely able to read and write in English. Fifteen percent of all ELLs scoring below basic had some sort of postsecondary education, including 8 percent who had attended a vocational or business school. Three percent had an associate's or other two-year degree, and 4 percent had university undergraduate or advanced degrees. Non–Spanish speakers reported higher levels of education than Spanish speakers. So while only 12 percent of Spanish speakers scoring below basic had some level of post-secondary education, 26 percent of non–Spanish speakers had some postsecondary education, with about 10 percent indicating that they had at least a college degree.

The apparent contradiction between holding a college degree and scor-ing below basic on English literacy may be because those who reported hav-ing completed college may have done so outside the United States in a language other than English. Adults with degrees from foreign universities, particularly those who have been in the United States for a short amount of time, may still be in the early stages of acquiring English literacy and on a forward trajectory in terms of English language development. The relatively small group of those who scored below basic in literacy but had higher edu-cational levels may also have included older immigrants, who received their degrees overseas but have lived in "linguistically isolated" neighborhoods where they did not have the opportunity to develop their literacy skills in English. Nevertheless, they may have been able to work and thrive in an ethnic community where English literacy skills were not necessary to make a living.

Of much greater concern in terms of program planning and policy are those English language learners who have not had the opportunity to com-plete high school in either the United States or their home country and who may be stalled in their literacy development. Since a high correlation exists between literacy skills in any language and schooling, we can assume that this group lacks the underlying reading concepts (such as phonemic aware-ness and decoding skills) associated with literacy development. If undered-ucated ELLs in this group do not attend ESL classes specifically designed to build literacy (either in English or in the first language), their economic opportunities are likely to be limited and job prospects negatively affected, increasing the odds that they will live in poverty.

New Directions for Adult and Continuing Education • DOI: 10.1002/ace

Labor Force Participation. In spite of very low levels of English literacy, a significant number of English language learners are working. Only one-third of all ELLs who scored below basic are not in the labor force, although the number is higher for ELLs born in the United States (55 percent). Spanish speakers had slightly higher labor force participation rates. Seventy percent of Spanish speakers, compared to only 58 percent of non–Spanish speakers with below-basic prose literacy, were in the labor force. As these numbers indicate, low literacy skills in English are not necessarily an impediment to employment, although they limit access to well-paying jobs. Many adults may be out of the labor force for reasons that have little to do with their level of English. Women may stay home to run households or raise children, and the elderly may be at the end of their working lives. Immigrants who are both new to English and new to the United States may still be in the early process of cultural adjustment and may need some time before joining the workforce.

At first glance, the fact that half of the ELLs scoring below basic were not only in the labor force but had full-time employment may appear paradoxical. However, as previous studies have shown (Greenberg, Macias, Rhodes, and Chan, 2001), even those with low levels of English proficiency can find full-time jobs, particularly in employment sectors where the work is low-skilled and hands-on. In addition, many immigrants find employment in their own ethnic communities and work in their native language.

Mismatch Between Oral Proficiency in English and English Literacy Skills. The NAAL data support the notion that those who can understand and speak English (oral proficiency) do not necessary read and write English (literacy). For example, close to a third (31 percent) of the foreign-born who scored below basic in English literacy said they spoke English either "well" or "very well"—indicating a mismatch between oral and written proficiency in English. This mismatch was very strong for ELLs who were born in the United States. In this group, more than eight out of ten (81 percent) reported speaking English either "well" or "very well." These findings again underscore the need for literacy development for U.S.-born English language learners who may have close to native-speaker skills in terms of oral proficiency but have significant gaps in their reading (and most likely writing) abilities. It is not surprising that the U.S.-born Spanish-speaking group spoke English "well" or "very well," most likely owing to the fact that they attended U.S. schools. Even those who spoke a language other than English at home tended to develop social communication skills in English as part of their schooling and acquired the ability to communicate in English face to face or on the telephone. What is surprising was the number of U.S.-born ELLs who still struggle with basic English literacy and lack the reading skills generally required to interpret connected text or make sense of simple newspaper articles.

Proficiency in English Literacy. The differences between those with only minimal English literacy (below-basic) and those who are able to read

New Directions for Adult and Continuing Education • DOI: 10.1002/ace

Table 1.6. Employment Status of English Language Learners, by Performance Level of Prose Literacy

	Prose			
Employment status	Below Basic	Basic	Intermediate	Proficient
Not in labor force	33	29	20	14
Unemployed, looking for work	7	9	9	8
Part-time	11	13	14	15
Full-time	50	50	57	63

Note: Detail may not sum to totals because of rounding.
Source: U.S. Department of Education, National Center for Education Statistics. *National Assessment of Adult Literacy (NAAL)*. Washington, D.C.: Government Printing Office, 2003.

quite well and interpret a range of English texts (proficient) are stark. One would suppose that those ELLs who grew up in the United States and presumably went through the U.S. school system (Generation 1.5) would have relatively high levels of literacy, somewhat similar to those of youth and adults whose first language was English. However, this was not the case. Only 6 percent of U.S.-born ELLs could read English texts proficiently, compared to 15 percent of native English speakers. This once again highlights the need to pay attention to the literacy needs of the Generation 1.5 population.

Labor Force Participation, Prose Literacy Level, and Income. In spite of lack of literacy skills, adults scoring below-basic had labor force participation rates of about 40 percent. These rates rose as competence in English literacy rose. Of those scoring proficient in prose literacy, only 22 percent reported either not being in the labor force (14 percent) or being unemployed and looking for work (8 percent), compared to 40 percent of those who scored below-basic in prose literacy (see Table 1.6).

While being able to read in English at the proficient level seemed to have some bearing on labor force participation, English literacy had a far more striking effect on income (see Figure 1.3). Of those who scored below-basic, almost half (45 percent) had a household income below the poverty threshold, compared to only 6 percent of those who scored proficient in prose literacy. Conversely, 86 percent of ELLs who scored proficient in prose literacy had incomes above 175 percent of the poverty line, compared to only 25 percent of adults in the below basic group. Clearly, while it is possible to find employment even with relatively low levels of English literacy, economic opportunities remain limited for those who struggle with reading and writing in English. As these comparisons illustrate, adults with low literacy in English face much higher odds of living in poverty, although education and work experience seem to matter as well.

New Directions for Adult and Continuing Education • DOI: 10.1002/ace

Figure 1.3. Distribution of Household Incomes of English Language Learners, by Prose Literacy Level

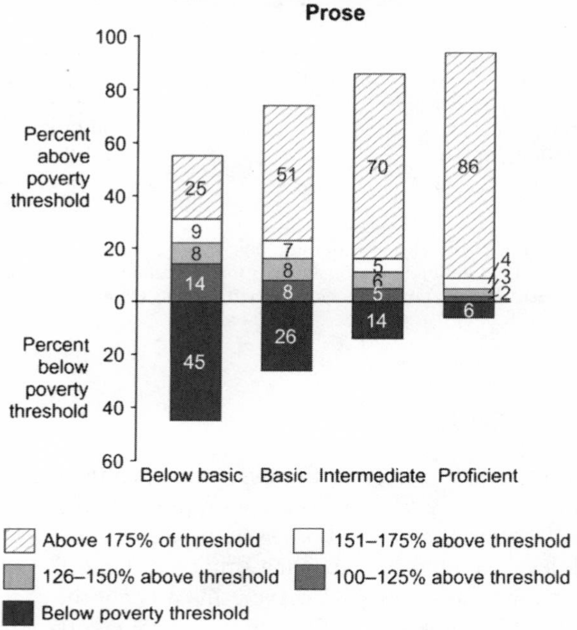
Prose
100
80
Percent above poverty threshold
60
40
20
0
Percent below poverty threshold
20
40
60
25
9
8
14
45
51
7
8
8
26
70
5
6
5
14
86
4
3
2
6
Below basic
Basic
Intermediate
Proficient
Above 175% of threshold
151–175% above threshold
126–150% above threshold
100–125% above threshold
Below poverty threshold

The Most Vulnerable Populations

For a number of reasons, literacy skills are not easily acquired, and difficulties in processing written information can be found in all groups, foreign- and U.S.-born, among English learners as well as among native speakers of English. Most English language learners do not (yet) have the English reading skills required to read the kind of lengthy and abstract prose that might appear in a newspaper editorial. They have difficulties integrating and synthesizing information from multiple sources of information, such as interpreting a table that lists blood pressure, age, and physical activity. NAAL data show that only about 28 percent of ELLs were able to perform the prose literacy tasks at the intermediate level and 6 percent at the proficient level.

Adults who have had only a few years of schooling are likely to struggle with literacy in any language, and acquiring literacy in a new language can be challenging. Given the predominance of Spanish speakers with low levels of both education and English literacy, two types of programs deserve consideration: literacy in the native language, to lay a foundation for the development of English literacy, and bilingual vocational programs that offer hands-on training but do not require strong English literacy skills to start (Wrigley and others, 2003).

Concerns About Generation 1.5. The younger members of U.S.-born ELLs who have high oral skills in English but weak literacy are part of Generation 1.5. This generation of bilingual ELLs have vocabulary and reading skills that may be insufficient to deal with informational texts written beyond basic levels and may have difficulties both reading and writing in English. If they did not receive education focused on academic literacy, they will most likely continue to struggle to succeed in contexts where strong English literacy skills are needed. This group of out-of-school youth and adults is of particular concern because their literacy skills are so low that they are not likely to make progress without intensive interventions focused on upgrading their academic skills, in terms of both background knowledge and reading and writing skills. Since they are highly proficient in oral English but still lack basic literacy, they are not easily served in conventional Adult Basic Education (ABE) or ESL classes. As a rule, the nonstandard writing styles these students exhibit, influenced by interference from their native language, is not addressed in ABE classes designed for native speakers of English, and their high proficiency in oral English puts them at odds with their LEP peers who attend ESL classes for the foreign-born.

Implications for Program Development

As the report on the NAAL by the National Research Council notes, literacy is an essential skill that helps individuals thrive individually, socially, and economically (Hauser, Edley, Koenig, and Elliot, 2005). English literacy is important to all aspects of life, from handling personal affairs to engaging in the workforce and participating in a democratic society.

Why should we worry about the English literacy of English language learners? Won't ELLs become literate in English as they interact more with others? The answer is yes for some and no for many others. We know that many newcomers who are literate in their native language do improve their English literacy skills as they advance in their general English learning and are supported either by classes or through independent reading and exposure to print.

However, natural language acquisition over time may not happen for foreign-born immigrants who have been in the United States for many years without having learned to read and write in English. These individuals are likely to have reached a learning plateau in terms of literacy and may not improve their literacy skills on their own without education or training that provides intensive experience with written English. Those who have low levels of education in their home country and so are likely to have weak literacy skills in their native language may be doubly disadvantaged. They may not be able to develop their reading skills on their own because they lack the basic foundations in literacy needed for interpreting print in any language. They may have gaps in both meaning-making and decoding skills and may find most print information inaccessible, although they may be able to recognize popular logos and understand common signs and other forms of environmental print ("No Smoking," "Rest Rooms," "STOP"). This group is unlikely to succeed in conventional ESL classes where some degree of literacy in the native language is assumed (Condelli and Wrigley, 2008).

Planning and Practice at the Community Level

The NAAL data provide a framework for measuring literacy skills on the national level, but they also offer important information for designing and implementing community needs assessments and other community-based interventions. Such assessments can determine to what extent first- and second-generation immigrants have the language and literacy skills needed not just to survive but to thrive.

The data on educational achievement reported by the NAAL have important implications for policy and planning because past experiences with schooling significantly influence the acquisition of English literacy. The higher the education in the native language, the more likely the individual will develop literacy in the second language. This tends to hold true for all language groups, even those that do not use an alphabet, such as Chinese, or use a non-Roman alphabet, such as Russian or Greek.

As new immigrants increasingly come from poor countries with fewer educational opportunities, their level of education can provide insight into how much and what kinds of ESL services might be needed.

Future Assessments

Whether they are community-based or national, further assessments can be designed to provide an even richer language and literacy profile of ELLs of all types, including members of the first or second generation, immigrants or refugees, and authorized or undocumented individuals. To permit the creation of appropriate policies and programs, new assessments should seek to deal with the complex nature of literacy in two languages and take a closer look at both English literacy and literacy in the native language. Although conducting assessments on the myriad of languages spoken in the United States may not be feasible, conducting assessments in Spanish, the most prevalent language of those with low literacy skills, may be possible.

Gathering reliable data on oral proficiency in English should also be considered in place of merely relying on self-reports. New assessments should seek to measure demonstrated competence in speaking and understanding spoken English, building on currently available standardized assessments such as the Basic English Skills Test (BEST; Center for Applied Linguistics, 2008). A national assessment that measures oral communication skills in English (conducted with a subsample if a full assessment is not possible) will make it possible to compare self-reports of English with documented performance.

New data on native language literacy and oral proficiency in English, along with the results of currently collected English literacy and background information, can both guide educational planning and link it to the kinds of academic and occupational opportunities available for different groups. If, as a country, we want to develop instructional programs for different types of immigrants, the information contained in the NAAL is necessary but not sufficient. As the need for skilled workers intensifies, and because new entrants into the workforce are increasingly immigrants, we will need demographic, educational, and skills profiles of the jobs that promise mobility for adults who are not yet proficient in English.

Conclusion

The National Assessment of Adult Literacy has brought the relationship between English literacy, educational achievement, and household income to the forefront. It highlights the needs for policies and services not only for the foreign-born who come to the United States for a better life or because they have been uprooted by war or civil strife but also for those who were born in this country and whose English literacy skills need further development.

The relationship between literacy and income points toward the urgent need for interventions designed for different groups of English language learners, including those with very limited education and those whose academic degrees from their home countries are not recognized in the United States. An investment in educational programs that not only develop language and literacy skills but also capitalize on the experience and expertise of immigrants would mean not only an investment in new Americans but could also serve to strengthen communities and the nation as a whole.

References

Castro, M., and Wiley, T. G. "Adult Biliteracy and Language Diversity." In K. M. Rivera (ed.), *Adult Biliteracy: Social and Programmatic Responses.* Mahwah, N.J.: Erlbaum, 2008.

Center for Applied Linguistics. *BEST Literacy Technical Report.* Washington, D.C.: Center for Applied Linguistics, 2008.

Comings, J., Sum, A., and Uvin, J. *New Skills for a New Economy.* Boston: MassInc., 2001.

Condelli, L., and Wrigley, H. S. "The What Works Study: Instruction, Literacy, and Language Learning for Adult ESL Literacy Students." In S. Reder and J. Bynner (eds.), *Tracking Adult Literacy and Numeracy Skills: Findings from Longitudinal Research.* New York: Routledge, 2008.

Fermstad, S. *Immigrants, Persons with Limited Proficiency in English, and the TANF Program: What Do We Know?* Washington, D.C.: Center on Budget and Policy Priorities, 2003.

Greenberg, E., Macias, R. F., Rhodes, D., and Chan, T. *English Literacy and Language Minorities in the United States.* Washington, D.C.: National Center for Education Statistics, 2001.

Hauser, R. M., Edley, C. F., Jr., Koenig, J. A., and Elliot, S. W. (eds.). *Measuring Literacy: Performance Levels for Adults, Interim Report.* Washington, D.C.: National Academies Press, 2005.

Kutner, M., Greenberg, E., Jin, Y., and Paulsen, C. *The Health Literacy of America's Adults: Results from the 2003 National Assessment of Adult Literacy.* Washington, D.C.: National Center for Education Statistics, 2006.

Macias, R. F. "Inheriting Sins While Seeking Absolution: Language Diversity and National Statistical Data Sets." In D. Spencer (ed.)., *Adult Biliteracy in the United States.* Washington, D.C.: Center for Applied Linguistics and Delta Systems, 1994.

Martinez, T. E., and Wang, T. *Supporting English-Language Acquisition: Opportunities for Foundations to Strengthen the Social and Economic Well-Being of Immigrant Families.* Baltimore, Md., and Sebastopol, Calif.: Annie E. Casey Foundation and Grantmakers Concerned with Immigrants and Refugees, 2006.

McHugh, M., Gelatt, J., and Fix, M. *Adult English Language Instruction in the United States: Determining Need and Investing Wisely.* Washington, D.C.: Migration Policy Institute, 2007.

National Center for Educational Statistics. "National Assessment of Adult Literacy (NAAL)." 2003. Retrieved Nov. 20, 2008, from http://nces.ed.gov/naal/.

Rivera, K. M., and Huerta-Macias, A. "Adult Bilingualism and Biliteracy in the United States: Theoretical Perspectives." In K. M. Rivera and A. Huerta-Macias (eds.), *Adult Biliteracy: Sociocultural and Programmatic Responses.* Mahwah, N.J.: Erlbaum, 2008.

Sum, A. *Forces Changing Our Nation's Future: The Comparative Performance of U.S. Adults and Youth on International Literacy Assessments, the Importance of Literacy/Numeracy Proficiencies for Labor Market Success, and the Projected Outlook for Literacy Proficiencies of U.S. Adults.* New York: National Commission on Adult Literacy, Council for Advancement of Adult literacy, 2007.

U.S. Department of Education. No Child Left Behind Act (P.L. 107–110), Title IX, Provisions pt. A, sec. 910: "Definition." Washington, D.C.: Government Printing Office, 2002.

U.S. Department of Education, National Center for Education Statistics. *National Assessment of Adult Literacy (NAAL).* Washington, D.C.: Government Printing Office, 2003.

White, S., and Dillow, S. *Key Concepts and Features of the 2003 National Assessment of Adult Literacy.* Washington, D.C.: National Center for Education Statistics, 2005.

Wrigley, H. S. "Beyond the Life Boat: Improving Language, Citizenship, and Training Services for Immigrants and Refugees." In A. Belzer (ed.), *Toward Defining and Improving Quality in Adult Basic Education: Issues and Challenges.* Mahwah, N.J.: Erlbaum, 2007.

Wrigley, H. S., and Powrie, J. *Demonstrating What Works in Linking LEP Adults with "Good" Jobs.* New York: Public Private Ventures, 2008.

Wrigley, H. S., Richer, E., Martinson, K., Kubo, H., and Strawn, J. *The Language of Opportunity: Expanding Employment Prospects for Adults with Limited English Skills.* Washington, D.C.: Center for Law and Social Policy, 2003.

HEIDE SPRUCK WRIGLEY *is a researcher in adult ESL literacy and president of Literacywork International. She is also a fellow with the Migration Policy Institute in Washington, D.C., working with its Center for Immigrant Integration Policy.*

JING CHEN *is a senior research analyst at the Federal Statistics Program (FSP) of the American Institutes for Research (AIR).*

SHEIDA WHITE *directs the National Assessment of Adult Literacy (NAAL) and the National Assessment of Educational Progress (NAEP) Writing Assessment, two key assessments of the U.S. Department of Education.*

JALEH SOROUI *is the project manager of national and international assessment of adult literacy programs at the Education Statistics Services Institute (ESSI/FSP) of the American Institutes for Research (AIR).*

Based on adult second-language acquisition research and whole-language principles, this chapter describes some best practices for teaching adults in ESL classrooms.

Best Practices for Teaching the "Whole" Adult ESL Learner

David Schwarzer

Justin is a twenty-eight-year-old volunteer ESL instructor at a local nonprofit community program. In "real life," he is an accountant. As part of the orientation for new instructors, the community program provides the volunteers with twenty hours of training, during which they hand out the curriculum and a series of topics to cover during a four-month period. He will also inherit the former ESL instructor's grammar textbook. He will have a group of fourteen adult learners of five different nationalities and language backgrounds in his class. Justin will also learn that attendance is an issue at the language program.

This vignette presents a typical scenario for an adult English as a second language instructor working at a nonprofit English language program. What have other ESL teachers done that have worked? What do we know about adult second-language acquisition theory that can help Justin? How can he create a learning community in his classroom with this diverse and shifting learner population? In the following sections, I will illustrate how the ideas of "whole-language learning" can be used to answer these questions.

Brief Review of Adult SLA Research

For a long time in the area of second-language acquisition (SLA), we thought of second-language teaching in terms of four language skills: listening, speaking, reading, and writing. Speaking and writing were considered active

NEW DIRECTIONS FOR ADULT AND CONTINUING EDUCATION, no. 121, Spring 2009 © 2009 Wiley Periodicals, Inc.
Published online in Wiley InterScience (www.interscience.wiley.com) • DOI: 10.1002/ace.322

skills; listening and reading were viewed as passive skills (Celce-Murcia, 2001). This way of thinking has evolved as we look at language usage and communication as negotiation processes. What has come to be known as "communicative language teaching" (CLT) has eclipsed the four-skills approach. "By definition, CLT puts the focus on the learner. Learner communicative needs provide a framework for elaborating program goals in terms of functional competence" (Celce-Murcia, 2001, p. 18). However, focusing on achieving effective communication does not mean that teaching grammar is not important because "while involvement in communicative events is seen as central to language development, this involvement necessarily requires attention to form" (p. 25). It is important to keep a healthy balance between focusing on meaning and focusing on form. Process and product are important, and some class activities could focus just on meaning (for example, writing in a dialogue journal to share with a classmate), and some others could focus on grammar and form (for example, writing an essay and editing for correct language structure). As a matter of fact, several researchers agree that vocabulary development, learner motivation, and meaningful interaction are critical aspects in adult ESL learning (Bello, 2000; De la Fuente, 2002; Ellis, 1999; Gass, 1999; Krashen, 2003).

Research suggests that word knowledge is the first step to becoming a competent communicator in a second language (Coady and Huckin, 1997). However, knowing words is not enough; knowing word families is also an essential part of second-language vocabulary-building activities (Laufer, 1997). Teachers can help learners enhance their vocabulary in several ways. For example, Gass (1999) points out that "incidental vocabulary" learning (the vocabulary we acquire when we are doing something other than formal learning, such as watching TV in the target language) is an effective way of enhancing learners' vocabulary. Teachers can incorporate television shows into class assignments and initiate discussions of and draw vocabulary from programs that are of high interest in U.S. culture (such as *American Idol* or *Friends*) or programs the language learners themselves suggest.

Another way to help learners enhance their vocabulary is the use of extensive reading (Burt, Peyton, and Adams, 2003; Krashen 2003). Learners' vocabulary increases dramatically through extended reading and follow-up activities (Wesche and Paribakht, 2000). Reading texts that are interesting and challenging for the learners also has a powerful effect on their vocabulary development (Burt, Peyton, and Adams, 2003). Importantly, vocabulary in the second language (L2) seems to increase over time when learners engage with text in meaningful ways and are encouraged to actively negotiate its meaning with others (De la Fuente, 2002). This means that a part of the teacher's job is finding reading materials of high interest and relevance to the language learners' lives and making them a part of the group's conversation and vocabulary work. Doing this could enhance the adult learner's motivation to learn.

Motivation is "why people decide to do something, how long they are willing to sustain the activity, [and] how hard they are going to pursue it" (Dornyei, 2002, p. 8). In this respect, it is also important to remember that adult ESL students in community programs are a shifting population; they move and change jobs often, and their motivation to learn ESL also transforms and evolves with the changes they face in their lives outside the classroom. As stated by Dornyei and Kormos (2000), motivation is not static; it may change from day to day, from task to task, and from learning community to learning community. For example, "integrative motivation" (willingness to learn a new language in order to become part of a particular speaking community) and "instrumental motivation" (willingness to learn a new language to accomplish immediate goals and needs) are both important aspects of why adults try to learn languages (Gardner, 1985; Oxford and Shearin, 1994). Depending on the circumstances under which the adult learner migrated to the United States, the ESL instructor may find different responses to the new culture among learners that influence their approach to the new language. Some may not want to adapt to the new culture or are experiencing culture shock. Others may be adapting very well to the new living environment, culture, and community. Some adult learners are very motivated to learn ESL because they need it to communicate with their colleagues at work or to obtain a promotion, accomplish educational goals, help their children with school assignments, or just feel confident speaking the language of the community in which they live.

Teachers need to discover what motivates the learners to come to their classes and take on the very challenging task of learning another language. They can tap in to their learners' motivation to both improve language learning and enliven the class by identifying high-interest popular media in the form of television programs, films, newspapers, magazines, and even signs, billboards, and posters that the learners encounter in their day-to-day lives. They can also use scenarios relevant to the learners' lives, such as renting an apartment, trying to get a job promotion, or going to the emergency room. When adult learners see their English class as connected and helpful to their real lives, they are more likely to invest the effort it takes to attend class and to approach their out-of-class lives as a language-learning laboratory. Teachers can support this by identifying individual, pair, or group projects (Florez and Burt, 2001) of importance to their adult learners, particularly projects that identify and build knowledge about community resources and how specific institutional systems work, such as the school system, banks and mortgage companies, and the medical establishment.

The ultimate goal of learning a language is to be able to communicate and interact with the people that speak it. Interaction is what happens when two or more people exchange ideas and negotiate meaning in order to prevent "breakdowns" (Ellis, 1999). This does not mean that we should focus only on listening and speaking skills; teaching grammar, vocabulary, and pronunciation to adult ESL learners is equally important in preventing communication breakdowns (Finn-Miller, 2004). However, interaction is crucial, as it makes learners aware of the gaps between what they want to say and what their listener understands (Schmidt and Frota, 1986).

Building a community in the ESL classroom helps provide a safe environment where learners can interact and try out using the new language. When they interact in class, they receive comprehensible input and feedback from each other (Gass, 1997). As language instructors, we can build a setting in which adult learners can learn and practice communication strategies and tools such as paraphrasing in order to describe, questioning for clarification, drawing on linguistic and world knowledge in order to build meaning, and using sentence fillers (*well, I mean, you know,* and so on) in order to become successful language users. Having different group activities in the ESL classroom provides opportunities for them to learn and practice these strategies and use these tools with others. One way to help them is to have them work in groups and pairs. Research has shown that students produce more and longer sentences when they work in groups and pairs (Doughty and Pica, 1986), and we know that language is best learned when social interaction is occurring and learners use the new language for social communication (Lantolf, 2006).

Whole Language for Adult ESL Classrooms

Whole language implies that we look at adult learners as whole persons rather than just ESL learners. It asks us to see the learners in our classes as parents, spouses, employees or business owners, neighbors, churchgoers, and members of various communities. In other words, when we approach learners in our classes as whole persons, we view them as adults with accomplishments, responsibilities, relationships, personal histories, and hopes. Moreover, whole language encourages the teacher and the learner to look at language not in segments but as a whole. In whole language, all language skills are integrated, class participants learn about the cultures of their peers and their communities, social rules are openly discussed, and class activities incorporate the students' knowledge and talents. Seven basic principles support the whole-person approach to second-language learning and teaching (Schwarzer and Luke, 2001): a holistic perspective; authentic learning; curriculum negotiation; inquiry-based lessons; language learning, a developmental process; alternative assessment; and community of learners.

Holistic Perspective. Taking a holistic perspective means looking at language as a whole rather than approaching it in pieces, such as studying adverbs in isolated sentences or practicing verb conjugation out of context merely to memorize the endings. It means studying the language in context so that the learners experience it in a realistic way. It prescribes integrating reading, writing, listening, speaking, and cultural activities; reading a chapter of a book or an article from the newspaper instead of isolated paragraphs,

New Directions for Adult and Continuing Education • DOI: 10.1002/ace

sentences, or words; and listening to an entire segment of a news or reality program before breaking it down into short interactions, sentences, or vocabulary. It helps the learners develop an understanding of the whole and then allows them to examine the pieces after that. Think about the context within which the piece was written or produced. Who was the audience? Why did the author write it or the producers produce it? What does it say about life, society, or politics in the author's or producer's society or culture?

Authentic Learning. Authentic learning means to incorporate learning materials and learning experiences from the learners' daily lives. Use classroom activities that learners could use tomorrow or the next day in real life. Use your learners as authentic audiences to practice on before they venture beyond the class. Make sure that in-class learning activities represent both the cultural context of the learners and the cultural context outside the classroom. For example, if they come from Latin America, ask them to explain about their culture, holidays, and what they miss from their country and at the same time to request information about the American culture and holidays to an English-only speaker. Not only are they learning the culture of the United States, but they are at the same time bringing their own language and culture to people who have lived in the United States all their lives.

Curriculum Negotiation. Curriculum negotiation involves asking learners to participate in the decision-making process related to the curriculum they will study. You cover the "mandated" curriculum but also make room to address learners' learning needs and wants. Integrate, if you can, what is mandated with things the learners are interested in their daily lives. Providing options is a good way to start the negotiation. Creating a chart with learners' needs and wants for the class may be another way to recognize and subsequently incorporate what is important to them into the class.

Inquiry-Based Lessons. Inquiry-based lessons promote the development of inquiry skills in the classroom. Encourage learners to ask questions and pursue answers to them. For example, the instructor can elicit questions from the students about a text they have read together. The students can formulate possible questions they would like the author of the text to answer in an interview, or they can formulate questions to help them understand the text more fully and pose them to their classmates. When learners ask their own questions, learning becomes more meaningful to them, and they invest more in their learning.

Language Learning: A Developmental Process. Language learning is a process, and learners will inevitably make mistakes when they are actively learning. The goal is to make "better" and more sophisticated mistakes as the learners progress in their learning. Therefore, taking risks and making mistakes should be embraced. Also, remember that what learners can produce in English does not necessarily reflect what they know about the language. Part of your job is to provide contexts and tasks that will help them use what they know and identify and fill in what they don't know.

Alternative Assessment. Alternative assessment requires that learning be measured by means of various evaluation methods, not just standardized testing. Such alternative assessments as portfolios, anecdotal records, and videotapes of learner presentations are effective tools to assess learners' progress over time, and these techniques also provide learners with useful and actionable information about their own progress. It is important to look not only at the product but also at the learners' processes of language learning.

Community of Learners. It is important that adults in the ESL classroom feel welcome and accepted for who they are. Developing a sense of belonging to the adult ESL class is crucial. The instructor and the learners act in both roles—as learners and as experts—in such a community. Adult learners are more willing to invest in their learning and continue attending the ESL class when they feel welcome and part of a caring learning community.

Teaching the Whole Adult ESL Learner: A Few Practical Ideas

The following section suggests ways in which the principles of the whole-language approach can be applied in adult ESL settings.

Building the Classroom Together. Like a new house, the ESL classroom is empty before the instructor and the learners meet for their first class. The first step when you move into a new place is to take ownership of the place and make it comfortable and welcoming for you. This is also true of the classroom. When you meet for the first time, invite your learners to "build the classroom" with you. Invite them to bring or make their own furniture such as shelves to store and display material or students' work, picture frames, and learning materials for their new class. Provide opportunities for them to make the classroom feel more like home. Let them bring food. Often adult learners arrive to class after a full day's work and are tired and hungry. Share your family and culture, and encourage your learners to share theirs. This helps learners take ownership of the learning environment, and that feeling may spill over into their other learning responsibilities in the class. And by integrating the learners into your classroom, you are focusing on their strengths and acknowledging that they bring valuable resources to the learning environment.

Capitalizing on Learners' Expertise. Adult learners bring a lifetime of knowledge and experience to the ESL class. They bring specialized knowledge from their professions and occupations. It is not unusual for ESL learners to have practiced as well-educated professionals (doctors or teachers) or skilled tradespersons in their countries of origin. Capitalize on their strengths; you can help your learners become "expert of the week" and take turns making class presentations on their topics. These presentations will enhance their vocabulary skills in their areas of expertise while integrating all language skills in an authentic and meaningful setting. Other students in class as well as the instructor benefit from learning the new information provided by their classmates on health, nutrition, cooking, beauty, construction, and carpentry depending on their occupations and professions.

Creating Independent Learners. Adult learners should depend as little as possible on their instructor for learning. The instructor should be one of many resources available to them. One way to start building independence in the learners is to have class routines. When there are clear and relevant class routines, learners are more focused on learning, and learning anxiety diminishes. Even if the instructor is absent, they know what should happen in the different segments of the class. Having class routines does not mean having a boring class. It means having direction and a clear set of procedures and expectations for the learners. Part of the routines you may consider are setting learning goals, having hands-on learning activities, and implementing self-assessment. These routines need to be consistent. When adult learners set their own learning goals and monitor their own progress, they feel more independent. Independent learners are more motivated to learn and are therefore more likely to keep attending class. They are also developing the skills to continue learning the language when they are not in your classroom.

Extending the Classroom to the World. Field trips are a great way to connect the learning that happens in the classroom with the life that goes on outside of it. Adult ESL learners need to learn about the new culture in real-life situations, and it is important to remember that what ESL teachers may consider commonplace is all new for someone from another country. Visiting places such as the supermarket, the hospital, and the public library offers an array of learning opportunities for the adult ESL learner. With the help of the learners, you can make a list of places to visit and plan for tasks to be accomplished during those visits. Learners can also go by themselves as an assignment and report on the experience. To support language learning from these activities, the instructor can design short lessons as follow-up activities in order to integrate the language skills from the field trip experience. You can take advantage of the printed messages in the environments visited and explore those messages with the learners in class. Field trips are just one more way to connect the classroom to the community outside.

Acquiring New Literacy Habits. When adult learners are exposed to a variety of hands-on activities, they develop new literacy habits. Literate adults read for pleasure, search the Internet, read newspapers, and know how to access services offered in their community. Also, learners who are exposed to libraries, museums, and the Internet may develop a taste for books, music, and art. When the instructor encourages learners to acquire these new literacy habits, they are able to apply them in their daily literacy needs as adults.

Empowering Justin. As an "emergent" adult ESL instructor, Justin has a lot to learn; however, he also has a lot to offer to the field of adult ESL. He should be encouraged to attend conferences and professional development geared toward improving adult ESL teaching and learning. Justin (and other adult ESL instructors like him) needs to document the practical knowledge he acquires through teaching adult ESL learners and sharing what he learns with other instructors. This practice will help him gradually develop his professional voice as an adult ESL instructor. By taking the risk to try new methodologies that look at the adult learner as a whole as well as by presenting them to his peers, he will develop and empower himself and other instructors. By turning his language classroom into a site of human interaction, by viewing language, learning, and teaching as holistic processes, and by inviting learners to bring their lives into the classroom while he brings his in as well, Justin forges a community that is not only good for language learning but also for the well-being of Justin himself, the learners, and the larger world.

Conclusion

Justin and other emergent ESL instructors teaching adult ESL learners should be praised for their commitment. They have stepped forward as members of their communities to share their language and thereby help those who have arrived more recently to find their place within the diverse richness of the many smaller communities that make up the whole of the nation.

References

Bello, T. *The Importance of Helping Adult ESL Learners Set Goals.* Washington, D.C.: Clearing House for ESL Literacy Education, 2000. (ED 445562)

Burt, M., Peyton, J. K., and Adams, R. *Reading and Adult English Language Learners: A Review of the Research.* Washington, D.C.: Center for Applied Linguistics, 2003.

Celce-Murcia, M. (ed.). *Teaching English as a Second or Foreign Language.* Boston: Heinle, 2001.

Coady, J., and Huckin, T. (eds.). *Second Language Vocabulary Acquisition: A Rationale for Pedagogy.* Cambridge: Cambridge University Press, 1997.

De la Fuente, M. J. "Negotiation of Oral Acquisition of L2 Vocabulary: The Role of Input and Output in the Receptive and Productive Acquisition of Words." *Studies in Second Language Acquisition,* 2002, *24,* 81–112.

Dornyei, Z. *Teaching and Researching Motivation.* Essex, England: Pearson, 2002.

Dornyei, Z., and Kormos, J. "The Role of Individual and Social Variables in Oral Task Performance." *Language Teaching Research,* 2000, *4,* 275–300.

Doughty, C., and Pica, T. "'Information Gap' Tasks: Do They Facilitate Second Language Acquisition?" *TESOL Quarterly,* 1986, *20,* 305–325.

Ellis, R. *Learning a Second Language Through Interaction.* Philadelphia: Benjamins, 1999.

Finn-Miller, S. "Pronunciation and the Adult ESL Learner." *Fieldnotes for ABLE Staff.* Retrieved October 24, 2008, from http://www.able.state.pa.us/able/lib/able/fieldnotes04/fn04eslpronunciation.pdf.

Florez, M. C., and Burt, M. *Beginning to Work with Adult English Language Learners: Some Considerations.* Center for Adult English Language Acquisition, 2001. Retrieved July 17, 2008, from http://www.cal.org/caela/esl_resources/digests/beginQA.html.

Gardner, R. C. *Social Psychology and Second Language Learning: The Role of Attitude and Motivation.* London: Arnold, 1985.

Gass, S. M. *Input, Interaction, and the Second Language Learner.* Mahwah, N.J.: Erlbaum, 1997.

Gass, S. M. "Discussion: Incidental Vocabulary Learning." *Studies in Second Language Acquisition,* 1999, *21,* 319–333.

Krashen, S. D. *Explorations in Language Acquisition and Use.* Portsmouth, N.H.: Heinemann, 2003.

Lantolf, J. P. "Sociocultural Theory and L2: State of the Art." *Studies in Second Language Acquisition,* 2006, *28,* 67–109.

Laufer, B. "The Lexical Plight in Second Language Reading: Words You Don't Know, Words You Think You Know, and Words You Can't Guess." In J. Coady and T. Huckin (eds.), *Second Language Vocabulary Acquisition: A Rationale for Pedagogy.* Cambridge: Cambridge University Press, 1997.

Oxford, R., and Shearin, J. "Language Learning Motivation: Expanding the Theoretical Framework." *Modern Language Journal,* 1994, *78,* 12–28.

Schmidt, R., and Frota, S. "Developing Basic Conversational Ability in a Second Language: A Case Study of an Adult Learner of Portuguese." In R. Day (ed.), *Talking to Learn: Conversation in Second Language Acquisition.* Boston: Newbury House, 1986.

Schwarzer, D., and Luke, C. "Inquiry Cycles in a Whole Language Foreign Language Class: Some Theoretical and Practical Insights." *Texas Papers in Foreign Language Education,* 2001, *6,* 83–99.

Wesche, M. B., and Paribakht, T. S. "Reading-Based Exercises in Second Language Learning: An Introspective Study." *Modern Language Journal,* 2000, *84,* 196–213.

DAVID SCHWARZER is associate professor at the University of Alabama, Birmingham. He teaches reading in multilingual settings.

New Directions for Adult and Continuing Education • DOI: 10.1002/ace

3

This chapter focuses on journal writing in adult ESL as a practice to promote literacy development and community building.

Journaling in an Adult ESL Literacy Program

Clarena Larrotta

The following excerpt describes the essence of keeping a dialogue journal with adult English as a second language (ESL) learners. "Dialogue journals are written conversations in which a learner and teacher (or other writing partner) communicate regularly (daily, weekly, or on a schedule that fits the educational setting) over a semester, school year, or course" (Peyton, 2000, p. 3). Federico (not his real name), an adult ESL learner in an intermediate class, reports on his experience with the dialogue journal:

> The dialogue journal activity is good—it is personalized. I have not written so much in English before, and at the very beginning I was scared. *The more you write, the more mistakes you make,* and that scared me a little. Before, I just used to write a paragraph or two, and now I write twice that amount. I still make mistakes; however, I know you will understand and you will answer. . . . I have learned to express things like I have done this and that— and you give me the opportunity to repeat those structures in the new letter. . . . It has been more effective for me because I talk about myself. . . . The answer you give me helps me identify mistakes, and I check for the right way of expressing ideas in English. . . . Through the journal I have learned basic structures also, and when I ask you questions, your answers are punctual. . . . This is another way of repeating the language structures.

NEW DIRECTIONS FOR ADULT AND CONTINUING EDUCATION, no. 121, Spring 2009 © 2009 Wiley Periodicals, Inc.
Published online in Wiley InterScience (www.interscience.wiley.com) • DOI: 10.1002/ace.323

As an ESL instructor, I have tried different writing strategies to engage adult learners to write in English for authentic communication, and the dialogue journal (DJ) activity has been the most effective. I implemented the DJ activity in my class as a volunteer English instructor in an adult literacy program in central Texas.

Dialogue journals are used in a variety of educational settings, and the literature on them is vast (Bardine, 1995; Brown, Sagers, and LaPorte, 1999; Peyton, 2000; Peyton and Staton, 2000; Wilcox, 1997). Teachers who have implemented the DJ in their classes report that reading the learners' entries and responding to them is a pleasant activity. Through writing back and forth in the journal, they get to know the learners, and all participants reflect on what they are teaching and learning. The DJ is a tool for teaching communication, increasing language fluency, and enhancing the learners' motivation to write in ESL (Holmes and Moulton, 1997; Huber, 2008; Larrotta, 2008). The goal with the DJ is to provide a space for the learners to express themselves freely writing in English; this activity is not intended to serve as an evaluation tool. The writing produced in the DJ is unique because everyone's journal is different, and it reflects the connections the learners make between language and thought.

It also provides the learners with opportunities for incidental vocabulary acquisition; in other words, they learn new vocabulary without realizing it.

Implementing the Dialogue Journal in the Adult ESL Classroom

Federico, Pablo, Flora, and Arturo (all pseudonyms) are four of the seventeen adult learners enrolled in an intermediate ESL literacy class. The group was made up of eleven male and six female learners between the ages of twenty-one and forty-three. They were carpenters, beauticians, salesmen, housewives, cooks, waitresses, and construction workers and came from different Spanish-speaking countries. We implemented the DJ as a weekly correspondence, writing back and forth in a notebook. For the implementation of the journal, I followed four steps: providing a model, collectively establishing guidelines, doing guided practice, and assessing the DJ activity.

Providing a Model. I wrote a letter introducing myself and gave it to all the learners. I finished the letter with two questions to guide the learners' response. They took the letter home and wrote their individual answers to my letter. I collected the notebooks in class and wrote individual entries to respond to each learner. We kept doing this the entire semester, and I continued modeling correct English structures while responding to the learners' entries.

Collectively Establishing Guidelines. We established guidelines together in class. For example, we agreed that we were going to include two questions each time to ensure that the other person had something new to say in the new entry. We committed to ask respectful questions and to have the right to refuse to answer questions that we thought were not appropriate or too personal. Instead we would suggest another topic for the written response. We also agreed that there was no length limit for the writing. We would write as much as we needed in order to follow the conversation and have a dialogue. Establishing these rules together was important for all of us, both to gain commitment to them and for learners to realize that as adults they also participate in the curriculum decision-making process.

Doing Guided Practice. I did not correct mistakes in the learners' entries because one of the goals of implementing the journal was to build a good rapport with the ESL learners. Instead of marking up their mistakes and providing the correct English version, we discussed their questions about language usage one on one. The goal of the DJ activity was to develop fluency writing in English, not to help them use correct English in their first attempt to communicate an idea in writing. We did other writing assignments to work on correctness (for example, guided compositions). In the journals, as their instructor, I modeled correct English structures in my entries. I also did mini-lessons in class on grammar, language functions, and word choice, addressing language issues that I had observed were common in the journal notebooks.

Assessing the DJ Activity. The learners reflected on their performance in writing the dialogue journal. I had asked them to make a list of the things they liked and disliked about keeping the journal. In general, learners liked the conversational and informal style of the journal. They also enjoyed reading my entries because they were individual and personal. The learners did not like that I did not correct their mistakes as I did in other writing assignments. Some learners said they had difficulties coming up with questions at times. As the instructor, I was satisfied with the results of implementing the DJ activity in the ESL class. It allowed me to observe learners' progress by comparing the quality and length of their journal entries. The DJ also gave me direction about the grammar topics I needed to review in class because I saw the patterns in the mistakes that the students were making.

Flora's DJ Entries

The following journal entries illustrate the process implementing dialogue journals in our class. I have chosen to share my DJ exchanges with Flora because she was the quietest learner in our group and her English was somewhat below the level of other learners in class. I want to illustrate that the DJ activity can be implemented in multilevel ESL classes. This was an intermediate ESL class, but she was more of a beginning language learner. However, this was not an impediment to our communicating in writing in English because we knew that the other person was trying to converse and communicate meaning.

New Directions for Adult and Continuing Education • DOI: 10.1002/ace

In the DJ entries, it was a common practice for us to use expressions in Spanish in parentheses in order to avoid interrupting the flow of the written message. We thought this was acceptable because we also switch back and forth between Spanish and English in our daily verbal interactions with other bilingual people. Also, using the learner's first language in the process of developing the second language benefits the acquisition of the second language because cognitive processes transfer from one language to the other and the learner makes connections between language and thought (Cummins, 2000; Jiménez, 2002). All journal entries were originally handwritten in a notebook.

Hello teacher Clarena:
    Congratulations, you achieve your goals, your doctoral study.
    Thank you for your class in English. I would like speak English for (ser)[to become] professional.
    My family lives in Mexico. I call them in week and weekend, (o sea) my father and mom and one sister but is very big my family. I have 5 sisters and 4 brothers. Total is ten but my other family is my husband and my daughter. Name of daughter is Dora of my husband is Pablo. (Adoro) [I adore] my daughter. I have a lot many nephews in here and in Mexico but now I live in Texas with my husband and my daughter one brother and one sister.
    Teacher tell me your favorite relative who is? and Colombia?
    Thank you. Bye
    Sincerely Flora

Hi, Flora:
    Thank you. My purpose when coming to Texas was to do doctoral studies, and I am almost finished. It is really exciting (emocionante) for me ☺!
    You adore your daughter. I understand that ☺! I love my nephew Diego. He is my favorite relative. He lives in Colombia. I don't have children, and I love him as if he were my own child.
    I am from the coffee region in Colombia. All my family lives there. Colombia is a green country with beautiful landscapes (paisajes). I think it is similar to Mexico in many ways; however, we eat "arepas," not tortillas, and we do not eat hot, spicy food.
    What professions do you like? What do you want to become?
    What do you do in your free time?
    See you in class,
    Clarena.

Hello:
    Teacher Clarena: Is good for you finish your doctoral studies.
    When I lived in Mexico in high school I remember I liked nurse. but now I live in Texas and my (propósito) [goal] is become executive chef.
    When is birth of your nephew?

Diego is son of your sister or your brother?
In my first day in your class not like but now is fine.
My free time is good. I am with my daughter in my free time.
Yes Mexicans love tortillas and spicy food. What is arepa?
I know your not married but when you get marry how many children you like to have?
Have good day.
I will be watting (*esperando*) your answer (*contestación*).
Bye.
Flora.

Wow! Flora, executive chef sounds good☺! According to what you have told me in class, you and the chef at work are good friends. I guess you do like this profession. Where can you study to become an executive chef? What are the requirements?

People say that an arepa is like a thick tortilla (*gordita?*).

My nephew's birthday is on January 18 ☺. Diego is my youngest sister's son. He is her only child. I am not planning to have children, but if it happens (*si pasa*), I would like to have only one child.

On a different note, I am glad you explained to me about your feelings in respect to our class (*me alegra que me explicaras tus sentimientos respecto a la clase*). Now I understand. Thank you for talking to me about this during the break. I am happy you decided to stay in class with us☺!
Write soon,
Clarena.

The dialogue journal is interactive; it is a dialogue or conversation between two participants, the learner and me, the instructor. The two participants write their entries in the same notebook. As illustrated in Flora's journal entries, our written conversation evolved with time, and we conversed about topics relevant to our lives. Communicating through the journal helped us continue conversations that we started in person but could not finish due to constraints of time or the intervention of other class members or people from the program. Flora's limited English did not prevent us from having an adult conversation in writing. We avoided ever implying that we did not understand each other because we were at different language levels. We became equally excited about keeping the correspondence because there is a certain magic in receiving a letter or written message from another person. The more we conversed, the closer we felt, and as the distance that often is inherent in the teacher-learner power relationship became weaker, we learned more from each other.

Learners' Comments on Keeping a Dialogue Journal

The following remarks made by the learners in the midterm class evaluation describe their perceptions of keeping a dialogue journal in our evening ESL class:

New Directions for Adult and Continuing Education • DOI: 10.1002/ace

"The journal is good. I have freedom to express my ideas and to write in the everyday language I use when I speak. I like reading your letters answering my questions." (Federico)

"With the journal we get to know each other at a more personal level, and I can propose topics for us to converse." (Pablo)

"I can ask you questions and talk to you about things and the others don't know what we are talking about. It's between you and me; this is why I like the journal." (Flora)

"The letters we share are not boring. It is the first time I write so much in English. I write and I wait for your response and that is fun." (Arturo)

The comments made by the learners provide a glimpse into the role of the teacher in the DJ activity. She acts as a more experienced partner to the learner, one who will provide correct language structures and more complex language in order to challenge the learners to extend themselves in this nonthreatening environment. She needs to be flexible and tolerant of learners' mistakes. She has to give up power and her desire to correct every mistake the learner makes. The DJ enables the learner and the teacher to build a relationship of friendship and trust.

DJ writing was an appropriate learning activity to do with this group of adults because it allowed me to work individually with the multilevel language learners that I had in my class. Even though this was an intermediate ESL class, Federico was an advanced learner, Pablo and Arturo were intermediate, and Flora was a beginner. For a learner like Flora, who was too shy to talk in class and had beginning language skills, the journal provided the opportunity to "talk" as much as she wanted and to reflect on how to say something and experiment with the language without the immediate reaction of a listener. Also, the DJ activity enabled learners to learn at their own pace. Yet at the same time I was able to work with Federico, an advanced learner who wrote longer journal entries, used sophisticated vocabulary and complex language structures, and made more refined mistakes.

Another important aspect of the journal activity was that it provided the possibility for learners to draw on what they already knew about their lives, their cultures, and their experiences and expertise while carrying out the written conversations. This is what González, Moll, and Amanti (2005) call "funds of knowledge." Funds of knowledge are the bodies of knowledge developed socially and historically by households; they are valuable cultural and social resources that learners possess. Keeping a DJ with my adult ESL learners taught me that they have interesting lives and know many things that I do not know. They have specialized knowledge and are curious about the world around them.

Dialogic Approach Through DJ Writing

The journal promoted a "dialogic approach" to literacy (Fallon, 1995; Freire, 1970). In other words, all of us were engaged in a genuine, two-way

New Directions for Adult and Continuing Education • DOI: 10.1002/ace

conversation. We responded to each other's journal entries and sometimes expanded on these messages orally by discussing further what we wanted to communicate to the other person. We experienced the essence of dialogue: we had the intention to communicate, anticipated a response, created knowledge about each other's world, and used generative themes in our correspondence; in sum, we kept a continuing, sustained dialogue (Fallon, 1995). In the words of Paulo Freire, "The word is more than just an instrument which makes dialogue possible. . . . Within the word we find two dimensions, reflection and action. . . . A true word is to transform the world" (1970, p. 87). The word is the instrument we use to communicate with each other. In our dialoguing, we constructed and reconstructed reality together using words. The dialogue was meaningful for both learner and teacher.

As noted, one element of our dialoguing together was that we developed generative themes. Generative themes "contain the possibility of unfolding into . . . many themes, which in their turn call for new tasks to be fulfilled" (Freire, 1970, p. 102). Generative themes are rich, complex topics, central to adults' lives and about which they want to express their views of the world and their realities. The generative themes for the learners in our class were immigration, employment, and culture. These themes provided a rich context around which our dialogues could happen and were central to the learners' realities, were relevant to their lives, and did not have to be appropriate to their language level. Using these generative themes, the participants in our dialogue learned about each other's reality and went beyond their own realities in order to gain a more comprehensive view of a topic and the world. Generative themes can be thought of as fundamental to dialogic teaching, but they are not the same as learners' interests: "Generative themes resonate with students, and using these themes as the basis of literacy education helps them [the adult learners] to connect with the written word" (Fallon, 1995, p. 143). The use of generative themes promotes true dialogue: "It can move people to wonderful new levels of knowledge; it can transform relations; it can change things" (Wink, 2000, pp. 47–48). In our intermediate adult ESL class, the journal served as a channel to open up the dialogue we needed in order to make community possible.

Building Community Through the DJ

The written conversations in the DJ helped our group grow as a learning community in that "communities are built on an understanding that students learn by actively constructing, rather than simply acquiring, knowledge" (Harada, Lum, and Souza, 2002, p. 66). The learners suggested the conversation topics, asked the questions they wanted to ask, and conversed using the topics that were relevant to them as adults. We, learners and teacher, connected as human beings and shared personalized discussions that we did not have in class because we were busy attending to program and curricular needs. Learning in community shaped the learning experiences as a negotiation process in which "the instructor brings experiences and understanding about learning and about students [and] students, in turn, bring their own interests and experiences" (p. 66). Thus the notion of community served our group in building solidarity, affection, emotion, and caring for each other (Flender, 2006), and the DJ activity promoted social interaction among us. It promoted free expression of ideas, learning about each other's cultures, and sharing and learning with others (Kim, 2005). The writing produced through the DJ activity was simply "good conversation"; it was interesting, functional, and continual, and it covered different topics (Peyton and Reed, 1990).

The journal was a springboard for us to build relationships. We know that community building happens through establishing personal connections and creating relationships (Sergiovanni, 2000). The DJ helped us build community in different ways. Through writing and subsequent oral interactions generated by journaling, we got to know about the life and needs of the individuals in the group. The learners and their instructor planned group activities as a result of these interactions. We identified commonalities and differences among the people in the group. We learned to respect one another and to look at each other as people who have knowledge and skills that not all of us shared. In an environment where community is present, "the class becomes more inclusive and builds a sense of unity. Students and teacher get to know each other and feel safe to express themselves, disagree, and even be vulnerable with one another" (Allen, 2000, p. 6). In the journal entries, learners asked questions and shared details of their personal lives and their many concerns in trying to adapt and succeed in the American culture. They wrote about family activities, personal goals and plans, hobbies, movies they saw, and their challenges and successes at work. Of course, I did the same; I reciprocated because I was a participant, not just the instructor. We were people interacting and communicating in genuine dialogue.

Lessons Learned Using Dialogue Journals with Adult ESL Learners

My teaching practice with adult learners is based on the idea that "pedagogy is the process of teaching and learning together. It is fundamentally about human interactions, the joy of playing with new ideas, and the challenge of integrating those ideas in the real world" (Wink, 2000, p. 59). The first time I used the DJ activity in my classes, I wanted to learn about the actual implementation of journaling in the adult ESL classroom, and I wanted my learners to benefit from this idea. By implementing the journal correspondence with my learners, I learned a lot about myself as an ESL instructor. I realized that as a teacher, I had been controlling the topics of the compositions too much and was not providing my learners with enough opportunities to experiment with writing and with language structures and self-discovery of the written word. I was not providing a true space for my learners to experiment with writing and feel safe doing it.

Throughout the implementation of the journal, I became more flexible and more tolerant of the learners' writing mistakes. Examining the mistakes that they made in their journal entries allowed me to design mini-lessons to target what my teaching experience told me were their particular learning needs instead of just following the order of topics established in the course syllabus as provided by the literacy center. I learned to let go and that I do not need to correct all the mistakes my learners make in their writing. I also learned that not all writing that learners produce needs to follow the steps in the writing process (drafting, revising, and editing). I needed to learn this in order to provide a true opportunity for the learners to gain fluency in writing in English and to foster the notion of independent learners. I have learned that long-term projects like the DJ activity serve as a means to get to know more about the learners as individuals and build an environment of community in which we can learn together.

References

Allen, T. "Creating Community in Your Classroom." *Education Digest*, 2000, 65(7), 6–10.

Bardine, B. A. *Using Writing Journals in the Adult Literacy Classroom: Teacher to Teacher.* Washington, D.C.: U.S. Department of Education, 1995. (ED 386596)

Brown, C., Sagers, S., and LaPorte, C. "Incidental Vocabulary Acquisition from Oral and Written Dialogue Journals." *Studies in Second Language Acquisition*, 1999, 21, 259–283.

Cummins, J. *Language, Power, and Pedagogy: Bilingual Children in the Crossfire.* Clevedon, England: Multilingual Matters, 2000.

Fallon, D. "Making Dialogue Dialogic: A Dialogic Approach to Adult Literacy Instruction." *Journal of Adolescent and Adult Literacy*, 1995, 39(2), 138–147.

Flender, L. "Others and the Problem of Community." *Curriculum Inquiry*, 2006, 36(3), 303–326.

Freire, P. *Pedagogy of the Oppressed.* New York: Continuum, 1970.

González, N., Moll, L., and Amanti, C. *Funds of Knowledge: Theorizing Practices in Households, Communities, and Classrooms.* Mahwah, N.J.: Erlbaum, 2005.

Harada, V. H., Lum, D., and Souza, K. "Building a Learning Community: Students and Adults as Inquirers." *Childhood Education*, 2002, 79(2), 66–71.

Holmes, V. L., and Moulton, M. R. "Dialogue Journals as an ESL Learning Strategy." *Journal of Adolescent and Adult Literacy*, 1997, 40, 616–622.

Huber, W. *Dialogue Journals: A Tool for Fostering ESL Writing Abilities.* Comptheory@UD [blog], Apr. 27, 2008. Retrieved Nov. 26, 2008, from http://comptheoryatud.blogspot.com/2008/04/dialogue-journals-tool-for-fostering.html.

Jiménez, R.T. "Fostering the Literacy Development of Latino Students." *Focus on Exceptional Children*, 2002, 34(6), 1–12.

Kim, J. "A Community Within the Classroom: Dialogue Journal Writing of Adult ESL Learners." *Adult Basic Education*, 2005, 15(1), 21–32.

Larrotta, C. "Written Conversations with Hispanic Adults Developing English Literacy." *Adult Basic Education and Literacy Journal*, 2008, 2(1), 13–23.

Peyton, J. K. *Dialogue Journals: Interactive Writing to Develop Language and Literacy.* Washington, D.C.: Center for Applied Linguistics, 2000. (ED 450614)

Peyton, J. K., and Reed, L. (eds.). *Dialogue Journal Writing with Nonnative English Speakers: A Handbook for Teachers.* Alexandria, Va.: TESOL, 1990.

Peyton, J. K., and Staton, J. *Dialogue Journal Bibliography: Published Works About Dialogue Journal Research and Use.* Washington, D.C.: National Clearinghouse for ESL Literacy Education, 2000. (ED 451731)

Sergiovanni, T. J. *The Lifeworld of Leadership: Creating Culture, Community, and Personal Meaning in Our Schools.* San Francisco: Jossey-Bass, 2000.

Wilcox, B. "Thinking Journals." *Reading Teacher,* 1997, *51*(4), 350–354.

Wink, J. *Critical Pedagogy: Notes from the Real World* (2nd ed.). New York: Longman, 2000.

CLARENA LARROTTA is assistant professor at Texas State University–San Marcos. She teaches in the Adult, Professional, and Community Education Program.

New Directions for Adult and Continuing Education • DOI: 10.1002/ace

English has a unique status in Puerto Rico, giving rise to special challenges in building community and teaching English as a second language on the island. Identity is at the core of these issues.

Identity Issues in Building an ESL Community: The Puerto Rican Experience

Betsy Morales, Eileen K. Blau

Whenever a second language is the object of learning, identity (or sense of self) is at stake, and the question of what community and what speech community one belongs to, strives to belong to, or is afraid to belong to raises complex issues. As stated by Zarate, Bhimji, and Reese (2005): "A bicultural identity is not necessarily a homogeneous or stable identity; nor is it a fixed location where cultures meet peacefully in perfect coordination" (p. 112). In Puerto Rico, we live in between two cultures, the Puerto Rican culture and the American culture. Therefore, English as a second language (ESL) instruction in Puerto Rico (PR) takes place in an unusual context. PR's history included language imposition, which has made issues of identity and community particularly delicate. In this chapter, we want to share some of our experiences teaching ESL in a society where language is directly linked to identity and political issues. We also want to discuss how our personal identities as a Puerto Rican (Betsy) and as a New Yorker (Eileen) and our understanding of community (where we live) influence our teaching practice in the ESL classroom.

Puerto Rico's Language History

Language is a controversial issue in Puerto Rico for two reasons: English was imposed on the island when the United States took possession of it in 1898,

New Directions for Adult and Continuing Education, no. 121, Spring 2009 © 2009 Wiley Periodicals, Inc.
Published online in Wiley InterScience (www.interscience.wiley.com) • DOI: 10.1002/ace.324

45

and as a commonwealth, the island's political status remains unresolved. In 1898, the United States attempted to enforce English as the sole language of instruction at all grade levels in PR. Unfortunately, the decision did not result in positive academic performance in schools and led to a half century of continuously changing practices. The standing policy since 1949 has been to use Spanish as the medium of instruction, with English taught as a required subject from the first grade. Puerto Rico is a free associated state or commonwealth, and Puerto Ricans are U.S. citizens, albeit without the right to vote in national elections (but also without the obligation to pay federal taxes). In spite of resistance, English has a strong presence on the island due to a number of factors, including decades of favorable tax incentives that have brought many U.S. companies to the island.

PR can be considered both an EFL- (English as a foreign language) and an ESL-speaking society (Blau and Dayton, 1997). People speak Spanish outside of school, and English is learned in formal education settings. The motivation to learn English is mainly instrumental (to accomplish a goal) rather than integrative (to belong to a culture). Students report that they learn English primarily to get jobs that pay well. Spanish is spoken at home and in informal and social interactions. Spanish is the language of higher proficiency (another EFL-like characteristic). English is encountered in textbooks, products, cable TV, magazines, and other media.

The ESL Students We Serve

The young adult population we serve at the University of Puerto Rico-Mayaguez (UPRM) is heterogeneous with regard to language proficiency. Some of our students are single parents with adultlike responsibilities. Some of them work at full-time or part-time jobs in order to pay for their education. In general, our students are a Spanish-speaking population with strong loyalty to their first language (Pousada, 2000; Vélez, 2000). The fact that most, if not all, of our students share the same native language is an important factor in the ESL classroom. Some surveys that we have conducted in the English Department show that in general, students have less confidence speaking English than using the other three language skills (listening, reading, and writing), both upon entering the university and at the end of their bachelor's degree. Research has repeatedly shown that most students hold more or less positive attitudes toward the language, but with stronger instrumental than integrative motivation (Irizarry-Vicenti, 2005; Lladó-Torres, 1984; López, 2007).

Our Personal Stories

As mentioned previously, in Puerto Rico we live in between two cultures: the Puerto Rican culture and the American culture. Our personal stories constitute a perfect example of this assertion.

New Directions for Adult and Continuing Education • DOI: 10.1002/ace

Betsy's Personal Account. I am a Puerto Rican born in New York and raised in New Jersey; however, at the age of ten, we moved to PR, and I became fully bilingual in Spanish and English. I earned my bachelor's and master's degrees in English education, gained some experience teaching ESL, and came to the United States to obtain a Ph.D. in multilingual education. When I finished my doctorate in 1999, I returned to my PR community and started teaching at UPRM, where I am currently the director of the English Department.

I usually teach intermediate ESL and public speaking. For me, the first step in teaching a class is to help the students get to know each other. I think of the classroom as the process of creating a "family" so that both the students and I can enjoy coming to class. Creating a sense of belonging among the students is important because they become more engaged and invested in their learning, and we cultivate this sentiment among the professors as well. As a Puerto Rican, family (*la familia*) is a priority for me, and I bring this cultural value to the ESL classroom. Two other important values reflected in my teaching practice are respect (*respeto*) and passion (*pasión*). I work long hours, pouring all my energy into my job in the ESL classroom and working with my colleagues in the English Department. I think we have the moral responsibility to get better at our work with each class and each semester, since all the students enrolled at the university are required to pass through our ESL program.

Eileen's Personal Account. I was born in New York, but Puerto Rico has been my home for the past twenty years. My career as a language teacher began as an English teaching fellow at a binational center in Honduras during the audiolingual era of language learning that was common a quarter of a century ago. During a second teaching fellowship in Uruguay, I worked with teachers, not so much as a teacher trainer but as a teacher of advanced ESL for competent non-native-speaking (NNS) teachers, who were eager for even greater competence. Both experiences of living in foreign countries were very positive, and I seemed to have found my calling. Professional training in TESL (teaching English as a second language), linguistics, and education (M.A. and Ph.D.) followed, and rather than being a chore, a few years in graduate school meant doing what I loved: being a student. This turn of events was the perfect way to satisfy wanderlust and a sense of adventure with a rewarding career.

After completing graduate work in 1980, I joined the faculty of the English Department at UPRM. I brought with me positive experiences of teaching several well-motivated populations, my own standards as a conscientious and enthusiastic student, and my awareness of how difficult it is to fully master a second language. I had studied Spanish and lived in Spanish-speaking countries and had quite a solid knowledge and reasonable fluency, but I was by no means a near-native speaker. I did not grow up in a Hispanic culture, nor did I have the later-in-life advantage of marrying a native speaker of Spanish to serve as a live-in informant and teacher, so the

New Directions for Adult and Continuing Education • DOI: 10.1002/ace

domains in which I used Spanish were much more limited than those of a native speaker. My expectations for students were that they would be motivated hard workers (like myself and like students I had had in the past), but I knew better than to expect complete accuracy in using their second language. In other words, my expectations for them reflected my own achievements and limitations.

Factors Affecting ESL Teaching and Learning in PR

Puerto Rican students value English with regard to their future professional lives but may not fully appreciate their need for it until later when they get a job that requires English proficiency or when they are transferred to the "mainland" United States (Echevarria, 2007). Motivation to learn the culture of the language is less strong but does extend to consuming popular culture using receptive skills such as listening to music in English, watching English-language TV on cable, and using the Internet (in both Spanish and English). This results in a sort of impersonal integration into North American culture.

Many students come to the university with a persistent fear of speaking English (McCroskey, Fayer, and Richmond, 1985). This fear weakens their motivation. Fear, coupled with resistance to English, makes it especially challenging to build community in ESL classes. Yet there is much more exposure to English in PR than in strictly EFL societies, and students do get input in English via music, cable TV, and the Internet. However, often many students are unwilling to turn this input to their academic advantage with regard to developing oral fluency, despite their perceived need for it. As in any educational setting, we have to make the appropriate pedagogical choices so that our students can form a community of successful language learners. Though our teaching approaches and techniques are not unique, they are the ones that fit our situation and enable us to build communities that start in our classrooms and radiate out to the larger English-using and bilingual communities in PR. We will refer to these approaches and techniques in the following section while showing why teacher identity is an important factor to consider when building community in our ESL classroom.

ESL Teacher Identity and Classroom Practice

The identity of the ESL teachers has a big impact on how they deliver instruction. The knowledge of self as a Puerto Rican born in the United States and as a New Yorker who has adopted Puerto Rico as her home has been an asset for us to better serve our Puerto Rican ESL students. We share some of the experiences our students bring with them to class and that helps us understand who they are and how to help them be more successful learning ESL.

New Directions for Adult and Continuing Education • DOI: 10.1002/ace

Betsy's Personal Account. I am aware that my identity is reflected in my teaching. As a Puerto Rican raised in my early years in the United States, I had a difficult time learning Spanish when I went to school in Puerto Rico. At home, my parents had us speak Spanish, but it was not the formal Spanish learned in the Puerto Rican classroom. Therefore, when I went to school, I feared Spanish and felt intimidated by my peers. They were native Spanish speakers and trained in academic Spanish at school. This situation is exactly what I have observed with my Puerto Rican students. They fear speaking English, especially with their peers, although they have received twelve years of ESL in school before attending the college classes I teach. Spanish is their native language, and the thought of English always being imposed on them makes them feel intimidated by the language.

As a language facilitator, I try to create a comfortable learning environment to help my students feel at ease and encourage them to use English in the classroom and outside of it. I focus on their learning needs, such as learning how to deliver a presentation in English or preparing to go on a job interview in English, and I also keep in mind the community where we live. For me, a family environment in the classroom means one in which we care for each other and help each other learn so that everybody feels comfortable to speak English freely.

There is more English in the Puerto Rican environment than in EFL societies and plenty of Puerto Rican literature in English (for example, Nicholassa Mohr, Judith Ortiz Cofer, and Esmeralda Santiago all write in English), as well as movies that have a Hispanic connection, such as *The Blue Diner* and *Real Women Have Curves*. I use literature and films like these to connect English with students' cultural identity.

In the higher-proficiency-level classes, I use Puerto Rican writers such as Esmeralda Santiago to get students to read and write about culturally familiar topics. Like Nieto (2002), the well-known writer on multicultural education, I define culture as "the ever-changing values, traditions, social and political relationships, and worldview created and shared by a group of people bound together by a combination of factors (which can include a common history, geographic location, language, social class, and/or religion), and how these are transformed by those who share them" (p. 53). To use culturally relevant texts helps build community and strengthen my students' identity.

In the public speaking class, I draw on what González, Moll, and Amanti (2005) call funds of knowledge, the knowledge that the students already possess as functioning members of their life worlds and, in our case, the Puerto Rican culture. I also provide opportunities for the students to develop their "first speech," their personal voice and story. Students need to be able to present who they are by using prompts such as "What values describe you?" "What culture defines you?" and "What person close to you helped make you who you are?" Generally, they regard this activity as difficult because they need to concentrate on figuring out who they are. After

New Directions for Adult and Continuing Education • DOI: 10.1002/ace

their personal introductory speeches, students seem to have become more comfortable with English and with each other. They are on their way to forming a language-learning community using English.

Another oral class activity is the impromptu activity. The students pick a topic at random and speak on it for one minute. Their topics are often controversial, funny, and tricky and include local and global social and political issues. As the instructor, I facilitate the ensuing conversation as necessary. What is fascinating is how the students interact with each other in English, thereby cementing the English-learning community within the class.

In terms of teaching writing, we take advantage of Spanish-English cognates (words that have similar spellings and meanings), such as student/*estudiante*, auto/*auto*, and motivation/*motivación*. The students also incorporate the use of Anglicisms (words that have evolved from English to become Spanish words) in Puerto Rican Spanish. For example, Puerto Rican slang is infiltrated by English slang and has incorporated words such as *janguear* ("hang out"), *gufear* ("goof on, make fun of"), *chillin* ("chill out, relax") *bling-bling* ("jewelry"), and *munchies* ("snacks, food to munch on") (Ríos, 2006). Again, this is a common way of speaking outside the classroom, and students also bring this language to the ESL classroom.

Eileen's Personal Account. The research on Puerto Rican English, my awareness of my own limitations in acquiring a second language, my identity in Puerto Rico, and current thinking in our profession (more awareness and tolerance of multiple "Englishes" than twenty years ago) have all led to a somewhat more liberal attitude toward the "native norm." Language is a live entity and takes shape according to where we are and the community that speaks it. Betsy explained some of the nuances of the way that English is spoken and some of the language phenomena happening in PR.

My vision of my experience of language teaching in PR crystallized at the 2008 Teaching English to Speakers of Other Languages (TESOL) conference at Lia Kamhi-Stein's keynote presentation. Her talk, titled "Building Classroom Communities Through Teachers' Lived Experiences," was particularly meaningful to me as I was developing this chapter with Betsy. In telling her own story, Lia described how as an Argentine graduate student in the United States, it took time before she felt a sense of legitimacy in her classes and was willing to become an active participant. I thought of how I, a normally rather outspoken individual in my first and even in my second language in a small enough setting, have never had the nerve to speak my mind in the large forum of the Arts and Sciences faculty meetings at my university. My alternatives would be to speak as a nonnative speaker of Spanish or to speak in English. I wonder which of my dual identities holds me back? I do not feel fully integrated into the Spanish-speaking community of the university, but I do not want to be a total outsider and use English. Am I so different from my students, who are afraid to speak English? Kamhi-Stein shared with us at TESOL her sensitivity to her students' need to feel the legitimacy necessary to become active participants. She therefore called on her audience to create conditions to give our students a voice. For me, this means that it is my duty to create the conditions that will help students overcome their fears so that English can become the useful tool that they will need to create an identity as bilingual Puerto Ricans. This will enable them to gain entry into yet other communities, increasing their options in life while keeping their Puerto Rican identity intact.

At UPRM, I have worked mostly with lower-proficiency students. They are the ones who come with the most resistance to English because they did not become bilingual as children or their precollege instruction just didn't take, for whatever reason. Not all these students want to work as hard as I think they should to master a second language, and as freshmen, not all have a realistic awareness of the need for English in their future, despite paying lip service to it. I have had a hard time understanding the unwillingness to work that I perceived. Why else bother to go to college? I wondered. What good was a degree or a profession without a solid knowledge base?

When I started in 1980, the trend in methodology was to move away from the audiolingual method to cognitive code and soon to the various manifestations of communicative language teaching (CLT). The humanistic approach to language teaching à la Gertrude Moskowitz (1978) did not particularly appeal to me, though I dutifully covered it in the graduate-level course I taught on TESL methods. However, I noted the enthusiastic reaction of many of the Puerto Rican graduate students. Over the years, I continued to be demanding of my students in terms of quantity of work, attending class, and handing in homework, but at some point, I began to focus less on the "half-empty glass," and this helped diminish my frustration. Some sort of delayed reaction to my own experiences slowly informed and modified me as a teacher; I better understood students' resistance to fully appreciate the value of English in light of their educational history, the effects of the sociopolitical context of PR, and their lack of maturity.

Although I have not pulled my copy of Moskowitz's book off the shelf, my empathy with the fearful second-language learner has been growing, and I have focused more on approaches that my colleagues and I use that successfully break down barriers and form community in our context and with our students without threatening their Puerto Rican identity.

I have for many years realized that with the most intractable cases, breaking the ice privately outside of class helps. In some cases, we use what students write about in their journals as the basis for speaking, allowing these particularly fearful students to talk about something about which they have full command and ownership.

I also individually interview all of my students in my office. I do this in order for us to get to know each other better and for them to see that they can indeed carry on a conversation in English, with a native speaker at that!

New Directions for Adult and Continuing Education • DOI: 10.1002/ace

These interviews have been a turning point for shy students and have given me an idea of how much to expect from them in class. This has helped me bring them into the classroom community. When a novel is required, I have used a second interview as a real-life conversation between two people who have read the same book, providing them with a glimpse of the community of literate language users.

One of our colleagues has her students venture out into the wider campus community (and sometimes beyond) by requiring that they speak to native speakers of English outside of class. Students commonly report in their end-of-semester reflection that they were glad to have been forced to engage in this intimidating activity and that native speakers did not make fun of them and were helpful rather than judgmental.

Conclusion

In the classroom, many of us strive to create a comfort zone for building a sense of community that includes both teacher and students. We do this on day one by having students interview each other and share what they learn with classmates and the teacher, who communicates to the students that they are genuinely important to her and cares about what they say. Once established, the sense of community must continue throughout the term. One way of achieving this is to integrate ourselves into the communication that goes on, even within structured grammar lessons, which can include questions and answers for the purpose of real communication. Another way is to occasionally use Spanish, which has been shown to facilitate second-language acquisition (Cummins, 2000). Particularly if the teacher is a nonnative speaker of Spanish, students see their teacher using their language imperfectly, thus motivating them to dare to use English, their second language, albeit imperfectly. A little self-deprecating humor can help establish rapport and help build a classroom community.

The roads to building community in our classes are not unique or extraordinary, but they fit our situation and work with our students. We all find different ways to break down barriers to build rapport and create communities, depending on our own identities and our own personalities. But more important is that we strive to give our students a sense of legitimacy and voice, which allows them to venture out into the larger community of PR as an English-using society and even into English-native-language communities in the United States. Helping students become aware of their identities and the process they go through while participating in the larger conversation of what it means to be a Puerto Rican and an ESL speaker can (as explained by Ullman, 1997) give them tools to find ways to be heard and help them learn how to participate more fully both in the classroom and in their various communities and the world outside the classroom.

References

Blau, E., and Dayton, E. "Puerto Rico as an English-Using Society." In R. M. Hammond and M. G. MacDonald (eds.), *Linguistic Studies in Honor of Bohdan Saciuk.* West Lafayette, Ind.: Learning Systems, 1997.

Cummins, J. *Language, Power, and Pedagogy: Bilingual Children in the Crossfire.* Clevedon, England. Multilingual Matters, 2000.

Echevarria, D. "English in the Lives of Former UPRM Engineering Students." Unpublished master's thesis, English Department, University of Puerto Rico, 2007.

González, N., Moll, L., and Amanti, C. *Funds of Knowledge: Theorizing Practices in Households, Communities, and Classrooms.* Mahwah, N.J.: Erlbaum, 2005.

Irizarry-Vicenti, M. "Attitudes of Ninth Graders in a Rural Middle School in Yauco, Puerto Rico, Toward the English Language and the English Class." Unpublished master's thesis, English Department, University of Puerto Rico, 2005.

Lladó-Torres, N. "Puerto Rican Attitudes Toward English as a Second Language." *Educational Research Quarterly,* 1984, 8(4), 92–102.

López, Y. "Attitudes of Basic Track Students Toward English at the University of Puerto Rico at Mayaguez." Unpublished master's thesis, English Department, University of Puerto Rico, 2007.

McCroskey, J. C., Fayer, J. M., and Richmond, V. P. "Don't Speak to Me in English: Communication Apprehension in Puerto Rico." *Communication Quarterly,* 1985, 33(3), 185–192.

Moskowitz, G. *Caring and Sharing in the Foreign Language Class.* Boston: Newbury House, 1978.

Nieto, S. *Language, Culture and Teaching: Critical Perspectives for a New Century.* Mahwah, N.J.: Erlbaum, 2002.

Pousada, A. F. "The Competent Bilingual." *International Journal of the Sociology of Language,* 2000, 142, 103–118.

Ríos, A. "Style for Puerto Rican High School Students: A Teaching Unit Focusing on Informal Style and Slang." Unpublished master's thesis, English Department, University of Puerto Rico, 2006.

Ullman, C. *Social Identity and the Adult ESL Classroom.* Washington, D.C.: Center for Applied Linguistics, 1997.

Vélez, J. A. "Understanding Spanish-Language Maintenance in Puerto Rico: Political Will Meets the Demographic Imperative." *International Journal of the Sociology of Language,* 2000, 142, 5–24.

Zarate, M. E., Bhimji, F., and Reese, L. "Ethnic Identity and Academic Achievement Among Latino/a Adolescents." *Journal of Latinos and Education,* 2005, 4(2), 95–114.

BETSY MORALES *is a professor in and director of the English Department at the University of Puerto Rico-Mayaguez.*

EILEEN K. BLAU *is a professor in the English Department at the University of Puerto Rico-Mayaguez.*

New Directions for Adult and Continuing Education • DOI: 10.1002/ace

*This chapter provides an in-depth look at the nature of
community building in short-term ESL courses. Examples
of classroom practices are provided.*

Community in a Hurry: Social Contracts and Social Covenants in Short-Term ESL Courses

Rob A. Martinsen

Like many adult ESL instructors, I have felt firsthand the challenges of creating community in short-term courses. Through my experience, I have noticed that in order to successfully build community in short-term ESL courses, teachers need to lay a foundation for social contracts and social covenants from the first day of the course and then take consistent steps to strengthen these commitments throughout the course. In this chapter, I will briefly discuss the nature of social contracts and social covenants as a basis for building community in short-term ESL courses. I will then discuss the timely and consistent application of practices and techniques that can strengthen social contracts and social covenants in order to develop community in short-term ESL courses.

Social Contracts and Social Covenants in a Hurry

Making and keeping social covenants and social contracts is paramount to building community in adult ESL courses. Ideally, our efforts to build community should help students commit to participating in our courses for two reasons: what they get out of the course and what they can give to it.

On its simplest level, the narrative of social contracts consists of a student with a learning goal and a teacher who commits to helping the student

NEW DIRECTIONS FOR ADULT AND CONTINUING EDUCATION, no. 121, Spring 2009 © 2009 Wiley Periodicals, Inc.
Published online in Wiley InterScience (www.interscience.wiley.com) • DOI: 10.1002/ace.325

reach that goal. The teacher contracts with the student to provide teaching that will help the student meet that need, and the student, based on that expectation, commits to participating in the course. ESL students, particularly adult students, often come to class with the expectation that in return for their presence and participation, they will receive certain benefits. For example, students may have a desire to improve their employment and thus expect that the course will provide them with the linguistic skills necessary for a particular job. Their attendance and participation in some ways is based on a kind of economic quid pro quo, which lends itself to the businesslike metaphor of a social contract. In these cases, it is important for students to feel that they are moving toward those goals; if not, students will find another way to reach their goals or, perhaps more tragically, give up on them altogether. It is therefore important for teachers to structure the course in a way that will meet the needs of these students and fulfill the terms of the social contract the students and teachers enter into as they agree to participate in the courses. Because students come with these goals, teachers in short-term ESL courses need to quickly demonstrate to their students that the course will indeed meet their needs.

ESL courses, however, can also be approached through the narrative of social covenants. Sergiovanni (2000) explains that social covenants, in contrast with social contracts, bring people together because of a shared vision and ideals. Over the course of my career, many of my students have been motivated to learn English for economic reasons, but many students have also expressed desires to help their children with their homework, read a newspaper, make friends with their neighbors and other people in the community, or simply set a good example for their children by studying and improving themselves—in short, to bolster relationships with others and participate more fully in society.

When instructors structure their classrooms in such a way that students help each other gain linguistic proficiency both for personal gain and to help improve the world, class members enter into social contracts and covenants and ESL classrooms become communities. The question many instructors are left with is how to accomplish such lofty goals in as little as seven weeks.

Building Community: Social Contracts and Social Covenants on the First Day

To truly build community through social covenants and social contracts, teachers must develop a trusting relationship with their students (Sergiovanni, 1994). Such relationships are generally strengthened over time. However, in a seven-week course, time is the one commodity in short supply. Because of this, teachers in short-term courses should plan ways to create community before the course begins and take action to build community from the very first day of class.

The first and perhaps most important step in fostering community through social contracts and social covenants is for teachers to keep the commitments that they make to students. If students feel that they cannot trust their teacher, they will believe that they will receive neither the benefits of social contracts nor the moral treatment of social covenants. As a teacher, I once promised my students that I would return a particular assignment by a particular date. The date came and I had not finished looking at their work, but my students seemed understanding. "Next time," I promised. Next time came and for whatever reason I was unprepared again. This time when the students asked about the assignment, they were still understanding, but I also noticed a subtle sense of disappointment. We all occasionally forget things, but students know very quickly whether or not they are the teacher's priority. My experience has taught me that students notice when teachers meet those commitments and the sense of community in the classroom is likewise strengthened or weakened.

Contrast this negative example with the teacher who immediately attempts to establish trusting relationships from the very first day by making and keeping a commitment to the students. Toward the beginning of the first class, the teacher engages students in some conversational getting-to-know-you activities and states, "If everyone speaks only English for the next fifteen minutes, toward the end of class we can listen to a beautiful song in English. I think you'll really like it." The students seem pleased and agree to speak only English for the designated time period. The teacher moves around the class encouraging students. At the end of the fifteen minutes, the teacher congratulates them for their efforts, and they listen to the promised music. In this way, the teacher establishes trust with the students from the first day of class.

This example may seem too subtle to be of consequence, but students always take note, whether consciously or unconsciously. This foundation, built on trusting relationships, is further enhanced when teachers begin the cycle again at the end of the first class period and complete it during the second class meeting. For example, the teacher could explain to students at the end of the first class that the topic for the next class period is reading and understanding newspapers in English and ask students to bring a newspaper article with them to class. Then during the next class period, the teacher carries out a meaningful lesson using the articles that students have brought. This is an example of an implied commitment on the part of the teacher. Students assume that since the teacher has asked them to do something, it will benefit their learning and growth. By following through with this implied commitment, the teacher demonstrates to the students that their efforts and participation in the classroom are valued. Students also begin to realize that they can trust the teacher to follow through on plans and commitments. When students begin to trust their teachers in this way, they become more willing to follow the teachers' guidance and participate more fully in the learning process. Creating this type of trusting relationship as soon as possible is important in short-term courses because it allows community building to occur right from the start.

The foundation of trust that I've described here can be further enhanced as teachers learn students' names and take steps to ensure that students learn each other's names. In my experience, students need to begin to develop the relationships with their teacher and other students that form the basis of social covenants from the very first day of class. When teachers and students learn and use one another's names, it adds an element of individual concern to the trust that teachers must develop. Taking the time to get to know students' names and a little bit about their background can increase students' motivation and subsequent performance in the class (Freeman and Freeman, 2002). Without this type of individual connection, many students' participation in the course will gradually diminish until they simply fade away.

Learning students' names quickly is particularly important for reinforcing social covenants in short-term ESL courses. In courses that last a semester or more, teachers may give themselves the luxury of learning students' names through normal interactions during the course. The same tactic in a course lasting seven weeks would mean that teachers are just learning students' names as the course ends and thus losing a great opportunity to create a community of learners in their classroom.

One creative way to learn names and build community quickly is for teachers to take pictures of students on the first day of class and then create a class roster. They then allow the students to add a profile to the roster with the personal information that they want to share (in English). After adding the profiles, the teachers provide each student with a copy of the roster.

Teachers knowing students' names is an important first step, but if students do not know each other's names, a learning community cannot form (Sergiovanni, 1994). The class roster also helps in building community by allowing students to get to know other students. Because students receive a copy, they will have a chance to see other students outside of class, speeding the getting-to-know-you process necessary for strong communities to form.

When Adults Can't Attend: Creating Community Each Time We Meet

As an adult ESL teacher, I realized that developing social contracts and social covenants in short-term courses is difficult in part because many students are unable to attend regularly. In my first experience teaching ESL to adults, I worked with a group of colleagues from a community college to provide instruction in English as a second language to the employees of a grocery store chain. Classes were held in a conference room in the back of one of the grocery stores. On the first class day, I planned what I had hoped were engaging activities where we could start to get to know one another and mix language learning with community building. During the

New Directions for Adult and Continuing Education • DOI: 10.1002/ace

next class meetings, however, I became gradually more disheartened as fewer and fewer students attended. Employees would come the first day with the best of intentions, but conflicting work schedules, family duties, and other challenges meant that many students could attend only a small portion of the time.

Erratic attendance was also an issue when two colleagues and I volunteered as ESL teachers during graduate school at a nonprofit organization. This program worked like a fitness gym: students paid a small membership fee and dropped in any time the program was open to "work out" their English. Students studied on their own from a series of textbooks or other materials or participated in impromptu classes with volunteers. Attendance in this program was even more unpredictable than at the community college, where students had at least signed up for a course with a set schedule. Over time we realized that adult ESL students juggle many responsibilities that can make regular attendance extremely difficult.

With so few class meetings in a seven-week course, we worried that students would completely miss out on their opportunity to be a member of the learning community that we were trying to create. We also realized that in order to help all our students, those who were able to attend regularly and those who were not, we would have to structure our classes in such a way that students could be quickly brought back into the community and reengage in learning.

Our first challenge was planning. We found ourselves asking difficult questions. Should we plan as though all the students would be in attendance? If not, which of our students should we have in mind? Interestingly, as the courses progressed, we noticed a pattern emerging. Generally, a small nucleus of two to five students attended consistently. Other students' attendance would fluctuate over the length of the course; sometimes they would come for one week and then be unable to attend for two weeks.

Ultimately, the other teachers and I decided that if we didn't plan with someone in mind, none of the students' needs would be met (Martinsen, Hanesch, and Moreno, 2006). Focusing my planning on students who attended frequently also seemed to help build community. These students became more engaged in learning because they received lessons that were designed with their needs and interests in mind. I feel that making specific lesson plans for these students met our portion of the social contract to provide students with the types of learning that would help them meet their professional or other goals. In addition, students recognized that their teachers cared about them, helping create the types of relationships that shore up the moral commitment of social covenants. This practice also benefited the students who were able to attend less regularly. As these students' needs were met, the students who attended only occasionally could sense the community that had formed and felt at ease when they were present.

Like many teachers, I have also found that routines are very useful, particularly in my short-term courses that many students were unable to attend

New Directions for Adult and Continuing Education • DOI: 10.1002/ace

regularly (Freeman and Freeman, 2002). Routines seem to provide a sense of stability to life in the classroom by helping students know what to expect and how to act. Routines are also helpful because students who have not attended regularly have a sense of what to do and can use their time engaged in the learning community rather than figuring out how to approach a new activity.

The key to making a routine effective is the same as with the other techniques that have been discussed: implementing them early in the course and then practicing them with consistency throughout. During my short-term ESL courses, I started each class with a reading activity. Implementing this practice consistently from the beginning of the course had several benefits. Students who arrived late felt more comfortable coming since they could begin working right away without interrupting the class. Also, students who had not attended in quite some time were able to step back into the course quickly because they immediately knew what to do when they stepped into class. Following individual reading time with discussion of the reading in pairs further helped students who had not attended recently reconnect with the classroom community.

Performing introductions during every class meeting is another routine that helped strengthen community in my short-term courses. After the reading activity, we would repeat our names and listen as we shared anecdotes from our lives, especially anything related to learning or using English. This helped students linguistically as they practiced introductions and narrating in the past, but even more important was the sense of community that came from learning about each other's lives and efforts to practice English. As part of this activity, students often shared ideas or provided encouragement in overcoming anxieties and obstacles to learning. This pattern was formed at the beginning of the course but continued all the way through because learning and relearning names and sharing personal stories allowed all students, especially those who had not attended recently, to quickly plug back into the community, despite not having been able to participate in the course as regularly as they would have liked.

Perhaps an even more effective way to go about introductions is to have a student ask another student for his or her name and some information and then introduce that person to someone else. This allows students further communicative practice and gets students to know a few classmates even more personally than simply hearing a brief introduction delivered to the whole class. Consistently providing time for such activities is helpful in any class, but it is doubly important in classes that last as little as seven weeks with students who can attend only intermittently.

Methods for Building Community Quickly

Sergiovanni (1994) explains that trusting relationships are at the heart of social covenants. Teachers in short-term ESL courses must therefore find ways to develop relationships with students in spite of the time constraints they face. Many teachers, however, ask students to spend nearly all of the class time in relative isolation from one another. In settings where classes will have a semester or more together, students might still have an opportunity to get to know one another, but in short-term ESL programs, this will not take place unless the teacher takes specific actions to allow students to work together to promote mutual learning.

Many researchers and scholars believe that language learning is a social process and have begun to take the focus away from individual efforts and place more emphasis on how people learn language through a process of socialization (Morita, 2000). Consistently applying methods that encourage social interaction from the beginning of short-term courses allows students to form the relationships necessary for a learning community to form.

Task-Based Language Learning. Task-based language learning is one method that lends itself to community building. Task-based teaching asks students to use the target language to accomplish a specific goal or objective (Nunan, 1991). This requires students to come together to exchange information, make decisions, and negotiate meaning. This interaction is vital in creating community. Chickering (2000) discusses the idea of maximizing interactions during class meetings as one of the principles of creating community in the classroom. As students work together to complete tasks, they will naturally share personal information and begin to get to know one another.

While teaching in one short-term ESL program, the other teachers and I engaged in a role-play in which students sat around a table holding menus. One teacher acted as the waiter, and students were asked to decipher the menu (from a local diner) and place an order. We knew that this would be difficult for our students and they would have to work together to complete the task. They pored over the menu together and shared likes and dislikes about food and experiences with the new foods and culture in the United States, with the majority of the exchanges taking place in English. Students also asked questions regarding the menu, such as "What is an 'early bird special'?" Some of the questions were directed toward us as the teachers, but students answered many questions as they shared ideas among themselves. This was an effective activity for language learning and community building because students learned to complete a communicative task and developed a sense of camaraderie as they learned more about each other and helped each other negotiate meaning in the target language. Implementing such activities regularly was crucial to our success in building community during the seven short weeks that we held classes.

This rosy picture should be tempered with the confession that our task-based and other interactive activities did not always work out exactly as we had hoped. Sometimes we did not plan our tasks adequately and students could not see the point. At other times the tasks were too complicated or challenging, obliging students to strain to help each other understand the task, sometimes in English and sometimes in their native Spanish. In spite of these problems, the interactive nature of our methods meant that students spent most of the class time engaged in helping each other learn and thus fulfilling social contracts and social covenants. Had we chosen to use a grammar-translation approach or other method that did not involve student interaction, there would not have been sufficient time for students to form the relationships necessary for a learning community to emerge.

Social-Change-Based Language Learning. Language learning and community building can also be accelerated when students unite their energies to overcome a challenge or problem that affects not only them and other members of the class but society as a whole. When students engage in such activities, they are creating a social covenant in the classroom because instead of acting out of self-interest, they are working toward the greater good.

The threat of losing government funding provided the context for my first attempt at asking students to learn by working for a larger cause. Government funding for adult education is often a two-edged sword (ProLiteracy Worldwide, 2007). On the one hand, such funding can provide the means to offer a valuable service to society. On the other hand, what the government gives, it can take away, sometimes very quickly. At one point, a budget crisis faced by the state legislature put our entire program's existence at stake. For weeks, rumors circulated that the program might lose its funding and disappear. This led to problems of motivation among teachers and students, who questioned whether or not they should continue to put forth their best effort when the entire program could disappear within a few short weeks.

After discussing the situation, the teachers in the program decided to use the threat of losing funding as a teaching opportunity. Through the grapevine, most of the students had heard rumors about the dangers the program faced. In our classes, we clarified the situation. Then we asked students to write letters to legislators explaining how the program had benefited them and society and requesting that the lawmakers do everything possible to provide the program with the necessary resources.

I admit that I was hesitant to ask my students to become involved. I had never participated in such an activity and was concerned that my students would respond negatively. Would students be excited about an opportunity to effect a positive change, or would they be shy about their limited English abilities? Without knowing for certain, I imagined that some of my students were undocumented residents and wondered if they would feel that their status in the country would be endangered if they communicated directly with government officials.

My worries proved unfounded. The assignment turned out to be very meaningful and engaging. When I first explained the situation to my students, they seemed excited by the prospect of using their English skills to make a difference in the world. I could sense the serious reflection they engaged in as they struggled to express the importance of these issues. As I reflected later, I realized that such projects could be used to build community in short-term ESL courses. Other assignments and class activities had been engaging, but few, if any, elicited the intensity of thought that students showed while writing these letters. I believe that their sincere engagement stemmed from a desire to do something important for others, which is essential to the relationships and moral conduct at the heart of social covenants and community. I believe that if teachers in short-term ESL courses can implement a project that from the very start asks students to work together to use their language skills for the greater good, students will quickly form a tightly knit learning community.

Conclusion

Building the type of community described here is possible in short-term courses, but it does not happen by accident. In my experience, teachers who successfully build community in short-term ESL courses take intentional steps. From the outset of the course, they enter into social contracts and social covenants with their students by laying a foundation of trust. They get to know their students and consistently structure their classroom in such a way that students also develop relationships with one another. Throughout their courses, they use methods and plan activities that draw on students' desire to contribute to society and allow students to reach their personal goals.

Creating such a classroom is a true challenge. Teachers accept this challenge because they believe in the inherent worth of their students. During my personal journey as an ESL instructor, I have been struck by the diligent efforts and sincere desire for learning demonstrated by my students, often in the face of tremendous challenges and difficulties. Such students are worthy of our best efforts at building community in short-term classes despite the limits of time or other obstacles that we and they may face.

References

Chickering, A. "Creating Community Within Individual Courses." In B. Jacoby (ed.), *Involving Commuter Students in Learning.* New Directions for Higher Education, no. 109. San Francisco: Jossey-Bass, 2000.

Freeman, Y. S., and Freeman, D. E. *Closing the Achievement Gap: How to Reach Limited-Formal-Schooling and Long-Term English Learners* (2nd ed.). Portsmouth, N.H.: Heinemann, 2002.

Martinsen, R. A., Hanesch, S., and Moreno, K. "Teacher Research and Student Needs: A Recipe for Invention." In D. Schwarzer, M. Bloom, and S. Shono (eds.), *Research as a Tool for Empowerment: Theory Informing Practice.* Greenwich, Conn.: Information Age, 2006.

Morita, N. "Discourse Socialization Through Oral Classroom Activities in a TESL Graduate Program." *TESOL Quarterly,* 2000, 34(2), 279–310.

Nunan, D. "Communicative Tasks and the Language Curriculum." *TESOL Quarterly*, 1991, 25(2), 279–295.

ProLiteracy Worldwide. "Funding Cut for Adult Literacy," 2007. Retrieved January 5, 2009, from http://www.literacyvolunteers.org/news/index.asp?aid=260.

Sergiovanni, T. J. *Building Community in Schools*. San Francisco: Jossey-Bass, 1994.

Sergiovanni, T. J. *The Lifeworld of Leadership*. San Francisco: Jossey-Bass, 2000.

ROB A. MARTINSEN is an assistant professor of Spanish pedagogy at Brigham Young University in Provo, Utah.

This chapter addresses the complexity of providing work-place ESL by identifying patterns of "best practices" in the related fields of human resource management, adult education, and training and development, all of which have a stake in workplace ESL and the integration of immigrant workers.

Complexity and Community: Finding What Works in Workplace ESL

Ann K. Brooks

English as a second language (ESL) classes in the workplace address the needs of a variety of populations, from temporary to permanent immigrants, from those with little to no formal education to those with more, and from those with little workplace power to those with some formal and perhaps significant informal power in their workplace. They come from Central America (37 percent), Asia (26 percent), Europe (12 percent), and South America, the Caribbean, and other areas (24 percent) (Grieco, 2004). They often belong to communities of people from their home country within the United States and maintain close ties with communities in their home countries, forming transnational communities that cross national borders (Kyambi, 2005; Portes, 2000; Staring, 2000). They are welcomed with varying degrees of acceptance by their U.S. communities and workplaces (DeJong and Tran, 2001). In general, the more education and professional preparation immigrants bring with them, the more likely they are to have acquired some English competency before entering the workforce or even arriving in the United States and also the higher their salary (Chiswick and Taengnoi, 2007).

Twenty percent of low-wage workers and almost two-thirds of low-wage immigrant workers are not proficient in English, and most have had little formal education. This group is the most likely to be served by workplace ESL classes. According to the National Center on Immigration Integration Policy, as many as three million legal residents are in need of

New Directions for Adult and Continuing Education, no. 121, Spring 2009 © 2009 Wiley Periodicals, Inc.
Published online in Wiley InterScience (www.interscience.wiley.com) • DOI: 10.1002/ace.326

65

English-language instruction, and this does not include unauthorized immigrants, thought to consist of two of every five immigrant workers (Martinez and Wang, 2006). Unauthorized immigrant workers are routinely subject to minimum-wage and overtime violations, unsafe working conditions, discrimination, and retaliation for speaking up (Bernhardt, DeFilippis, Martin, and McGrath, 2005) and are the most likely to be isolated from both their native and U.S. communities.

Providers of ESL training vary as well. Given the differences in background and work contexts of different immigrant populations in the United States, it is not surprising that workplace ESL delivery models, when they exist, also differ. Most common are workplace-education partnerships, workplace-union partnerships, workplace employing its own program staff, workplace–private contractor partnerships, and workplace and community-based organization partnerships. Some of the issues and challenges facing workplace ESL programs are securing funding, involving all partners or stakeholders in all stages of programming, tensions between work-centered and worker-centered educational goals, a tension between transferable and customized language skills, funding accountability requirements, and the challenge many educators find in communicating effectively with business (Burt, 1997). Workplace-based ESL classes have the advantage of addressing language skills within the context of the job. However, apparently few employers offer ESL instruction, owing to scheduling problems, cost, the perception of little benefit to the organization, and the belief that the responsibility for ESL training lies elsewhere (Burt, 2003).

Chaos and Best Practices

The ideas of chaos and complexity are not new to language educators (Larsen-Freeman, 2008). But I first encountered them as a way of looking at work organizations (Cohen and Stewart, 1994; Connell and Nord, 1996). Applied to language, learning, and teaching, these ideas help us step outside of hardened dichotomies such as competency versus performance, individual speaker versus social interaction, and language-centered versus student-centered and critical approaches to teaching. They also remind us to keep sight of the whole of language learning while at the same time focusing on individual aspects (Larsen-Freeman, 1997). Applied to organizations, these ideas remind us to consider the unintended consequences of our actions, to think in terms of relationships instead of individuals, and to see how organizations are connected to, affect, and are affected by events in other organizations and nations. One key idea is that new forms and patterns emerge out of chaos and complexity. These ideas are useful here in that adult workplace ESL, with its multiple partners, erratic funding, and diverse providers, is a complex, even chaotic arena of practice. Out of this complexity, do any patterns that point us toward best practices emerge?

New Directions for Adult and Continuing Education • DOI: 10.1002/ace

In this chapter, I will examine the best practices among three separate but related groups of practitioners, each with a stake in the provision of workplace ESL education: human resource managers, adult ESL educators, and training and development professionals. Each group serves a different set of clients, has a different history, and brings a different perspective to workplace ESL. Each maintains its own community of practice (Wenger, 1998; Wenger and Snyder, 2000) with its own professional conferences, electronic mailing lists, journals and magazines, and history.

Human Resource Managers. Human resource managers serve the interests of their work organization, whether they be business, government, or nonprofit. For human resource managers, the point of workplace training is for employees to acquire particular skills, change specific behaviors, and enhance the ability to work well in a particular space. This applies to all training and development, whether it is an organization-sponsored management program or workplace ESL courses. The specifics of particular courses are relevant mostly in relation to the expected outcomes: Can the people who have been trained do what they need to do and work with the people with whom they need to work? In fact, according to the chief learning officer at Booz Allen Hamilton, "When top leaders at Booz Allen think about what constitutes training we're happy to pay for, . . . it's rarely an issue of ROI [return on investment]. It's more about return on expectations. . . . What [trainees] say when they return to work about the help they got from a course carries a lot of weight with higher-ups" (Gordon, 2007, p. 44).

What are workplace expectations for ESL training? An article in HR Magazine, the trade magazine for the Society for Human Resource Managers, alludes to these expectations and how they are being met by providing workplace training in workers' native languages: "Many employers are providing ESL language training. But those efforts, while admirable, fall short of the overall goal of developing a highly informed workforce. Some employers are starting to provide all workplace training in the employee population's native tongue, recognizing that cultural differences and gaps in English language proficiency reduce comprehension of training programs" (Tyler, 2005, p. 67).

This pragmatic shift to offering training in workers' native languages has been driven by a focus on productivity, quality, and workplace safety issues. One executive for a consulting firm that designs compensation plans explains, "In an English training session, Spanish speakers do not understand, are intimidated, and soon tune out. Many of the problems that employers have with their [Spanish-speaking] workers are due to the fact that no one ever explained anything to them in Spanish" (Tyler, 2005, p. 67). Other training providers, including consulting companies and community colleges, provide Spanish-language training for sexual harassment, job skill training, and safety instructions. Advice to those who offer workplace training in Spanish are to keep the training voluntary, allow workers to choose the language in which they would like to receive training, include the choice to attend both English- and Spanish-language sessions, do a thorough needs analysis of both language and culture needs, and prioritize training if you can provide some training only in ESL workers' native language (safety training, for example). Additional advice is to use qualified translators as opposed to bilingual supervisors to transmit information and training to Spanish-speaking employees to optimize the chance for workers to receive accurate information (Tyler, 2005).

One challenge work organizations face in offering ESL training is the variation in quality of external vendor programs, courses, and instructors. One study found that although employers liked hiring immigrants because of their work attitudes and productivity, English skills were often a problem. However, in several companies that did offer ESL classes, the ESL instructors taught grammar and vocabulary that were decontextualized instead of making the classes relevant to the workplace (Burt, 2007). Nevertheless, in spite of the absence of consistent quality in the classes, another study found that the return on investment for English-language classes in a candy manufacturing company was an error reduction and productivity increase of as much as 30 percent (Chenven, 2004).

In fact, human resource managers have their own ideas about what contributes to quality workplace ESL training. One article written for HR managers recommends that before offering ESL courses, they should

- Meet with supervisors or managers to find out whether they have witnessed any difficulties with English communication
- Observe employees while they work and look for communication difficulties as well as anxiety, insecurity, or frustration because of a lack of English mastery
- Make sure that immediate supervisors are a part of the process of deciding to offer English classes so that they continue to support it
- Present English lessons in terms of the workplace so that students can see the immediate usefulness of the training
- Use authentic materials
- Limit class sizes to groups of ten or twelve
- Schedule classes for two hours at least twice a week in the mornings or at the beginning of a work shift to increase attendance
- Run courses for at least three months but no longer than six months
- Offer courses at the worksite
- Make participation voluntary rather than mandatory
- Market classes so that non-native English speakers will know what is being offered and not expect too much too quickly, with a term of five years for attaining English proficiency being considered realistic (Tyler, 1999)

Most work organizations in the United States are interested in productivity, quality, and avoiding litigation. Workers who do not understand

New Directions for Adult and Continuing Education • DOI: 10.1002/ace

instructions, cannot communicate with their colleagues, and do not understand workplace policy can undermine any of these interests. English classes, training in workers' native languages, and the use of translators and interpreters are all pragmatic efforts to ensure organizational success.

Adult ESL Educators. Adult educators are first and foremost learner-centered educators. At times this makes funding their work difficult because they consider their clients to be the learners rather than the funders. Whereas most professional fields are permanently attached to one or more institutions that provide regular funding for their services, adult educators, for the most part, fund their work through grants or as a tangential part of an organization, such as a community college or the public schools. From the perspective of adult educators, ESL education should serve ESL learners, whether by providing them with the nuts and bolts of the language, helping them develop contextualized language identities, or teaching them how to critically analyze the social contributors to their oppression.

Recent research in adult ESL provides us with a list of "what works" for adult ESL learners in terms of both instruction and programming (Condelli, Wrigley, and Yoon, 2002). Regarding instruction, research yielded four recommendations. The first is to use "authentic" materials to improve basic reading skills. Adult ESL learners engage with language that is "real" in their lives. The second is, if possible, to use learners' native language for giving instructions and clarifying concepts, as this will improve their growth in both reading comprehension and oral communication. The researchers suggest that native-language use reduces learners' anxiety about not understanding, enables them to focus on the task instead of the instructions, and helps create a safe learning environment. They also note that native language use helps learners develop critical thinking skills that enable them to accomplish daily tasks (and I would add, critically analyze their social context). The third recommendation is to use various strategies for presenting new materials and practicing. This leads to improved oral communication skills and exposes ESL learners to English in its various contexts and usages so that they can better grasp "how English works" and what is appropriate in particular contexts. Finally, the fourth recommendation is to explicitly emphasize verbal skills to help learners improve their oral communication.

Regarding classes and programming, the researchers found that longer classes increase the development of oral skills and reading comprehension but reduce the development of reading skills. They also found, unsurprisingly, that regular attendance improves both reading comprehension and oral communication skills. In addition, more years of education improve growth in basic reading skills, and younger students develop basic reading and oral communication skills faster than older ones.

Additional advantages of ESL classes held in the workplace are that those held during the workday or immediately before or after work are easy for busy adults to attend; they are funded by the employer, a union, the U.S. government, or a foundation, so they are usually free of charge; instructors can make materials relevant and authentic; and a positive work environment can develop when native-speaker colleagues act as peer mentors or conversation partners and participate in the classes with their ESL colleagues. Potential challenges are that employers may nurture unrealistic expectations about how quickly ESL speakers can master English; learners may be intimidated by native-English-speaking coworkers; preparing customized workplace-specific materials is time-consuming for teachers; teachers and learners may be reticent to address sensitive workplace issues in workplace-sponsored classes; and ESL professionals may find that businesses' pragmatic "training" orientation conflicts with the more holistically conceptualized idea of "education" that they value (Burt, 2003).

This highlights a significant difference between human resource management and adult ESL educators: HR managers place a higher value on helping the organization achieve its goals than on educating the individual learners, whereas adult ESL educators value the individual learners above the organization.

Training and Development Professionals. Training and development practitioners are interested in training and developing individuals within the context of work groups and organizations. While they may seem to be indistinguishable from HR managers in that they "belong" to the organization, they are more likely to strongly emphasize the well-being of workers, believing that the workers' success contributes strongly to the organization's success.

One area of inquiry that is relevant to workplace ESL education is the transfer of training. Success in training transfer may be defined as the degree to which learners apply to their jobs the knowledge, skills, and attitudes gained in training (Holton, Bates, Seller, and Carvalho, 1997).

Three dimensions of workplace learning appear to affect the transfer of training from the classroom to the workplace: individual characteristics, job attitudes, and work environment (Baldwin and Ford, 1998). Individual characteristics relevant to ESL might include motivation, previous education, and ability; job attitudes might include identification or engagement with the work being performed or the workplace, personal sense of power or efficacy within the work context, and perceptions of coworkers; work environment might include support for English learning, respect for English learners, and respect for the English learners' native language and culture.

In one recent study of best practices (Burke and Hutchins, 2008), training experts most frequently named five strategies as contributing to successful transfer:

1. Supervisors' support and reinforcement, especially recognition and reinforcement for the use of new knowledge and skills on the job
2. Coaching and opportunities for practice, including time to practice the skills immediately upon returning from the training
3. Using interactive activities to encourage participation, such as collaborative activities, role-plays, and small group exercises

4. Evaluation of skills used after training
5. Using content during training that is relevant to actual job duties

Strategies 3, 4, and 5 correspond to the "what works" research on adult ESL (Condelli, Wrigley, and Yoon, 2002). However, strategies 1 and 2 suggest that for ESL learners to actually apply their learning to their work contexts, the organizational context needs to support the efforts of ESL learners to communicate at work.

A recent and significant shift in workplace training practice has grown out of problems with training transfer, resulting in the move away from learning in classrooms to learning in the actual work context. As opposed to formal classroom training, informal learning occurs when individuals make sense of their experiences in the context of their daily work lives. This involves both reflection and action and may include self-directed learning, mentoring, trial and error, networking, and coaching (Watkins and Marsick, 1992).

Learning in the work context seems to improve proficiency. Proficiency can be defined as the ability to skillfully apply knowledge within a particular domain (Scheckley and Keeton, 1999). Research suggests that those who are proficient in a certain domain have developed an extensive and well-organized base of knowledge that has been constructed through experience, and models of proficiency development place informal learning characterized by reflection and action as central. In fact, one study (Enos, Krhahn, and Bell, 2003) on managerial learning found that the most prevalently reported learning activity was "interactions with others." Those who advocate for a sociocultural approach to language learning would regard this as being true for ESL learners as well.

Patterns Across Best Practices

Several patterns important to the provision of adult workplace ESL emerge from the best practices identified in each of these fields. Perhaps the most important is that workplace ESL needs to be as relevant and as closely integrated with the actual work environment as possible. There are a variety of ways to integrate work and language learning, including the following:

- Recruit and train English-language and culture coaches and mentors at the worksite
- Develop bilingual written material such as signs and important on-site memos and directives
- Reconceptualize language classes as "reflective communities" in which ESL learners name the communication challenges they are facing and the language teacher serves as a reflective resource
- Reconceptualize classes as "meetings" or "forums" in which ESL learners with more workplace longevity address the group and share what they have learned

- Advocate for a bilingual workplace in which interested native English speakers have the opportunity to study and learn Spanish or other common workplace languages by finding ways to focus together on problems they are attempting to solve at work

One challenge for language teachers is to help students who come from different countries and cultures and who speak so many different languages. There seems to be a widespread assumption that Spanish speakers are the only ones who speak a language other than English in the workplace. Indeed, in certain states such as Texas and California, Spanish speakers do predominate. However, that is not always the case; for example in Ohio, in addition to Spanish speakers, there is a large group of immigrants from Somalia. In this case, perhaps teachers and students could obtain multicultural training to alleviate this situation.

ESL providers also need to attend to the membership and belonging needs of ESL speakers. Ways of doing this include gaining the support of supervisors, involving English-speaking colleagues as language coaches and peer mentors, and working to normalize and value the use of both English and other languages at the worksite. Another important pattern in best practices is to offer classes consistently and in a way that maximizes the chance that ESL learners can attend. Specifically, offer classes on-site, regularly each week, if possible before a worker's shift, and for about an hour and a half.

Conclusion

Workplace ESL providers are responsible not just for providing the basics of the language but also for helping integrate ESL learners at work. Effective integration of ESL learners requires that we not only enable and encourage them to draw on the competencies they have brought with them from their native language and culture but also to find ways to help them become more powerful and competent in English too. Best practices suggest that learning occurs within the community of work.

References

Baldwin, T. T., and Ford, J. K. "Transfer of Training: A Review and Directions for Future Research." *Personnel Psychology,* 1998, *41*(1), 63–105.

Bernhardt, A., DeFilippis, J., Martin, N., and McGrath, S. "Unregulated Work and New Business Strategies in American Cities." Paper presented at the 57th annual meeting of the Labor and Employment Relations Association, Philadelphia, June 2, 2005.

Burke, L. A., and Hutchins, H. M. "A Study of Best Practices in Training Transfer and Proposed Model of Transfer." *Human Resource Development Quarterly,* 2008, *19*(2), 107–128.

Burt, M. *Workplace ESL Instruction: Interviews from the Field.* Washington, D.C.: Center for Applied Linguistics, 1997.

Burt, M. "Issues in Improving Immigrant Workers' English Language Skills." ESL Resources: Digests, 2003. Retrieved July 3, 2008, from http://www.cal.org/caela/esl_ resources/digests/Workplaceissues.html.

Burt, M. *Workplace Instruction and Workforce Preparation for Adult Immigrants.* Washington, D.C.: Center for Adult English Language Acquisition, Center for Applied Linguistics, 2007.

Chenven, L. *Getting to Work: A Report on How Workers with Limited English Skills Can Prepare for Good Jobs.* Washington, D.C.: AFL-CIO Working for America Institute, 2004.

Chiswick, B. R., and Taengnoi, S. *Occupational Choice of High-Skilled Immigrants in the United States.* Bonn, Germany: Institute for the Study of Labor, 2007.

Cohen, J., and Stewart, I. *The Collapse of Chaos: Discovering Simplicity in a Complex World.* New York: Penguin, 1994.

Condelli, L., Wrigley, H. S., and Yoon, K. *What Works Study for Adult ESL Literacy Students.* Washington, D.C.: Aguirre International American Institute for Research, 2002.

Connell, A., and Nord, W. "Infiltration of Organization Science by Uncertainty and Values." *Journal of Applied Behavioral Science,* 1996, 32(4), 356–377.

DeJong, G. F., and Tran, Q. "Warm Welcome, Cool Welcome: Mapping Receptivity Toward Immigrants in the U.S." *Population Today,* 2001. Retrieved Aug. 8, 2008, from http://www.prb.org/Articles/2001/WarmWelcomeCoolWelcomeMappingReceptivity TowardImmigrantsintheUS.aspx.

Enos, D. M., Krhahn, M. T., and Bell, A. "Informal Learning and the Transfer of Learning: How Managers Develop Proficiency." *Human Resource Development Quarterly,* 2003, 14(4), 369–387.

Gordon, J. "Eye on ROI." *Training,* 2007, 44(5), 43–45.

Grieco, E. *What Kind of Work Do Immigrants Do? Occupation and Industry of Foreign-Born Workers in the United States.* Washington, D.C.: National Center on Immigrant Integration Policy, 2004.

Holton, E. F., Bates, R. A., Seller, D. L., and Carvalho, M. B. "Toward Construct Validation of a Transfer Climate Instrument." *Human Resource Development Quarterly,* 1997, 8(1), 95–113.

Kyambi, S. *Beyond Black and White: Mapping New Immigrant Communities.* London: Institute for Public Policy Research, 2005.

Larsen-Freeman, D. "Chaos/Complexity Science and Second Language Acquisition." *Applied Linguistics,* 1997, 18(2), 141–165.

Larsen-Freeman, D. "Does TESOL Share Theories with Other Disciplines?" *TESOL Quarterly,* 2008, 42(2), 291–294.

Martinez, T. E., and Wang, T. *Supporting English Language Acquisition: Opportunities for Foundations to Strengthen the Social and Economic Well-Being of Immigrant Families.* Baltimore: Annie E. Casey Foundation, 2006.

Portes, A. "Globalization from Below: The Rise of Transnational Communities." In D. Kalb and others (eds.), *The Ends of Globalization: Bringing Society Back In.* Lanham, Md.: Rowman & Littlefield, 2000.

Scheckley, B. G., and Keeton, M. T. *Ecologies That Support and Enhance Adult Learning.* College Park: University of Maryland, 1999.

Staring, R. "Flows of People: Globalization, Migration, and Transnational Communities." In D. Kalb and others (eds.), *The Ends of Globalization: Bringing Society Back In.* Lanham, Md.: Rowman & Littlefield, 2000.

Tyler, K. "Offering English Lessons at Work." 1999. Retrieved on January 5, 2009, from http://findarticles.com/p/articles/mi_m3495/is_/ai_58738506.

Tyler, K. "Clear Language/Claro Lenguaje: By Delivering Workplace Training in the Language Employees Understand Best, You Can Improve their Productivity, Compliance and Morale." 2005. Retrieved January 5, 2009, from http://findarticles.com/p/ articles/mi_m3495/is_/ai_n15976157.

Watkins, K., and Marsick, V. "Towards a Theory of Informal and Incidental Learning in Organizations." *International Journal of Lifelong Education,* 1992, 11(4), 287–300.
Wenger, E. *Communities of Practice.* Cambridge: Cambridge University Press, 1998.
Wenger, E., and Snyder, W. "Communities of Practice: The Organizational Frontier." *Harvard Business Review,* Jan.–Feb. 2000, pp. 139–145.

ANN K. BROOKS is a professor of adult education at Texas State University–San Marcos.

7

This chapter discusses underlying themes and emergent issues related to community building and the learning and teaching of adult ESL.

Final Thoughts on Community in Adult ESL

Clarena Larrotta

Community building is an important, if not essential, element of adult English as a second language (ESL) learning. Communities, whether civic, work, religious, or identity-based, are the contexts within which we cease to be alone and become connected with others. "Community offers the promise of belonging and calls for us to acknowledge our interdependence" (Block, 2008, p. 3). When adult learners feel that they belong to a place (the ESL classroom, the literacy program they are attending), they invest in their learning and take ownership of the curriculum. That is why the contributors to this volume consider that adult learning in general and language learning and teaching in particular happen best within the notion of "community."

Language is the main tool for communicating with others in our communities. For immigrants and adult English learners, language provides not only the bridge to basic survival but also the means by which they forge relationships with neighbors, colleagues at work, and the people who work in the shops, agencies, and institutions in their new country. Immigrating to a new country affects a person's social identity and requires a readjustment in many different areas of the person's life (Ullman, 1997), which is why it is so important that we build community in the language classroom.

Each of the authors in this volume contributes something different to the discussion on the importance of community building in the adult ESL classroom. Some authors contribute by telling about their teaching experiences and others by sharing some of the research they do. Together they examine the role of community as central to ESL learning and teaching,

New Directions for Adult and Continuing Education, no. 121, Spring 2009 © 2009 Wiley Periodicals, Inc.
Published online in Wiley InterScience (www.interscience.wiley.com) • DOI: 10.1002/ace.327

describing teaching strategies and exploring theories that can help adult ESL learners with this struggle to learn a new language and culture and integrate into the communities of which they have become a part.

Factors Influencing Adult ESL Teaching

It is crucial to understand who attends ESL classes and overcome the personal biases that instructors may hold toward adult learners in ESL programs. The contributors to the volume appropriately regard ESL learners as adults and advise that all instructors treat them as capable individuals and rise above any stereotypical illusions that these learners come from a background of poverty and illiteracy. Thus the authors of Chapter One set the context by describing today's immigrant population, detailing who they are and which language skills they possess and which they need to acquire. In Chapter Five, Rob Martinsen describes the importance of building trust with adult students as an effective means of developing and enhancing community.

In addition, this volume highlights the importance of using appropriate teaching strategies to engage adult learners, building community in the classroom, and opening up the boundaries of the classroom to help learners engage more fully with their communities. For example, Chapter Two explains how the whole-language approach can be used effectively in adult ESL instruction. Chapter Three describes the use of journaling.

Relevant ESL Classes

What happens in the classroom translates into the students' reality, their communities, and that reality is incorporated into class activities. The chapters in this volume add to the body of literature on adult ESL teaching and learning, emphasizing the importance of offering ESL classes that will provide useful information and learning that can be applied to the learners' daily needs in their jobs, families, small communities, and the larger social community. For example, in Chapter Six, Ann Brooks explains how to make workplace ESL classes relevant to workplace issues.

The volume also emphasizes the importance of looking at the effects that identity and culture have on ESL instruction. Chapter Four describes the direct impact of social, cultural, and political events of the community outside the classroom on community building inside the classroom. These are relevant issues to adult learners and their language training.

The Importance of Community to Adult Learners

This volume stresses that learning a language is not just an exercise in mastering isolated skills such as speaking, listening, reading, or writing. It is a process through which learners develop a new identity and a new understanding of the world that incorporates the new language. Because community building is important to adults, the language-learning transactions that occur in the classroom need to reflect both the complex community and culture-based identities of learners and instructors and the necessity of structuring language learning to incorporate the learners' need to belong to a community. Adult ESL learning can no longer be conceived of as occurring solely within the walls of the classroom.

Community Building as a Process

All of the chapters in this volume point to the concept of community building as a shared process that implies reciprocity and adults working together to negotiate meaning and share knowledge as effectively as possible. It is a developmental process, and the first step is to build trust among participants. It is important to keep in mind that community building happens when instructors and learners feel comfortable and safe with each other and collaborate in the classroom in such a way that they continue doing so when the class is over. Community reminds us of our responsibilities to the common good (Fendler, 2006). In the ESL classroom, the common good requires that all individuals in class learn to use English effectively in their various communities. Working in collaboration and working toward a common goal are also part of the process of community building.

Conclusion

This volume integrates knowledge about adult learning and adult ESL. It brings the important perspective of community to our work as language instructors and supporters of the newcomers to the English language and culture. While not attempting to provide recipes or claim to have a foolproof list of dos and don'ts for teaching adult ESL in the context of community, the contributors to this volume offer practical ideas and relevant theories born of their own professional experience in order to challenge readers to reflect on their own practices and beliefs. The editors and authors of this volume hope to inspire further conversations and encourage more discussion and knowledge sharing among adult ESL educators.

References

Block, P. *Community: The Structure of Belonging.* San Francisco: Berrett-Koehler, 2008.
Fendler, L. "Others and the Problem of Community." *Curriculum Inquiry,* 2006, *33*(3), 303–326.
Ullman, C. *Social Identity and the Adult ESL Classroom.* Washington, D.C.: Center for Applied Linguistics, 1997.

CLARENA LARROTTA *is assistant professor of adult education at Texas State University–San Marcos. She teaches in the Adult, Professional, and Community Education Program.*

INDEX

Adams, R., 26
Adult Basic Education (ABE) classes, 6, 21
Adult English language learners: age and newcomer status of, 16–17; assessing literacy skills of, 5–23; and comparison of Spanish-speaking English language learners and speakers of other languages, 13–14; comparison of, with foreign-born English language learners, 11–13; distribution of, by employment status, household income, and welfare participation, 11t; distribution of, by selected characteristics, 10t; distribution of, by self-reported oral English proficiency, educational attainment, employment status, and household income, 12t; and educational attainment levels and prose literacy performance levels by Spanish-speaking status, 13t; employment, income, and welfare participation in, 10–11; employment status of, by performance level of prose literacy, 19t; ethnicity, age, and educational attainment of, 9; scoring below-basic in prose literacy, distributed by years living in United States and age of immigration, 16t
Adult immigrants: age and newcomer status of, 16–17; assessing literacy skills of, 5–23; and comparison of Spanish-speaking English language learners and speakers of other languages, 13–14; comparison of, to U.S.-born English language learners, 11–13; data source for assessing literacy skills of, 8–11; distribution of, by employment status, household income, and welfare participation, 11t; distribution of by selected characteristics, 10t; distribution of, by self-reported oral English proficiency, educational attainment, employment status, and household income, 12t; employment, income, and welfare participation in, 10–11; ethnicity, age, and educational attainment of, 9; levels of English literacy of, 14–20

Adult Literacy Supplemental Assessment (ALSA), 9
Age, 9, 16–17
Allen, T., 42
ALSA. See Adult Literacy Supplemental Assessment (ALSA)
Alternative assessment, 30. See also Whole-language learning
Amanti, C., 40, 49
American culture, 45
American Idol (television program), 26
Arturo (pseudonymous; English as a second language learner), 36, 40
Asia, 65
Authentic learning, 29. See also Whole-language learning

Bakhtin, M., 1
Baldwin, T. T., 70
Bardine, B. A., 36
Basic English Skills Test (BEST; Center for Applied Linguistics), 22
Bates, R. A., 70
Bell, A., 71
Bellah, R. N., 2
Bello, T., 26
Bernhardt, A., 66
BEST. See Basic English Skills Test (BEST; Center for Applied Linguistics)
Best practices: and adult ESL educators, 69–70; chaos and, 66–71; and finding what works in workplace ESL, 65–72; and human resource managers, 67–69; patterns across, 71–72; and training and development professionals, 70–71
Bhimji, F., 45
Blau, E. K., 3, 45, 46; personal account of, 47–48, 50–52
Block, P., 2, 75
Blue Diner, The (movie), 49
Booz Allen Hamilton, 67
Breakdowns, communication, 27–28
Brooks, A. K., 4, 65, 76
Brown, C., 36
"Building Classroom Communities through Teachers' Lived Experiences" (Kamhi-Stein), 50

79

Burke, L. A., 70
Burt, M., 26, 27, 66, 68, 70

California, 72
Canada, 6
Caribbean, 65
Carvalho, M. B., 70
Castro, M., 5, 16
Celce-Murcia, M., 25–26
Center for Applied Linguistics, 22

Central America, 65
Chan, T., 18
Chen, J., 3, 5
Chenven, L., 68
Chickering, A., 61
Chinese language, 22
Chiswick, B. R., 65
Classroom: building, together, 30; extending, to world, 31
Coady, J., 26
Cofer, Judith Ortiz, 49
Cohen, J., 66
Comings, J., 6
Communicative language teaching (CLT), 26, 51
Community: importance of, to adult learners, 76–77; of learners, 30. See also Community building
Community building, 28; and creating community at each meeting, 58–60; methods for quick, 60–63; as process, 77; in short-term ESL courses, 55–63; and social contracts and social covenants in hurry, 55–56; and social contracts and social covenants on first day, 56–58; and social-change-based language learning, 62–63; and task-based language learning, 61–62; through dialogue journal, 41–42
Condelli, L., 22, 69, 71
Connell, A., 66
Cummins, J., 38, 52
Curriculum negotiation, 29. See also Whole-language learning

Dayton, E., 46
De la Fuente, M. J., 26
DeFilippis, J., 66
DeJong, G. F., 65
Dialogue Journal (DJ): building community through, 41–42; dialogue approach through writing, 40–41; of Flora, 37–39; implementing, in ESL classroom, 36–37; learners' comments

on, 39–40; lessons learned using, 42–43. See also Journal writing
Dillow, S., 9
Dornyei, Z., 27
Doughty, C., 28

Echevarria, D., 48
Edley, C. F., Jr., 21
Educational attainment: ethnicity, age and, 9; and literacy level in English language learners, 17; and prose literacy performance levels of English language learners by Spanish-speaking status, 13t
EFL. See English as a foreign language (EFL)
Elliot, S. W., 21
Ellis, R., 26, 27
English as a foreign language (EFL), 46, 48, 49
English as a second language (ESL), adult, 21; factors influencing teaching of, 76; and journal writing, 35–43; relevant classes in, 76; whole language for, 28–30
English for Special Purposes, 14
English language learners: and concerns about Generation 1.5, 21; most vulnerable populations of, 20. See also Adult English language learners
English literacy levels: and comparing English language learners with below-basic English literacy skills to those who are proficient, 15–16; comparing, of English language learners with native speakers of English, 14–15; differences in, 14; of English language learners, 14–20; future assessments of, 22–23; and implications for program development, 21–22; and income, 19; and labor force participation, 18; mismatch between oral proficiency and, 18; and planning and practice at community level, 22; and proficiency in English literacy, 18–19
Enos, D. M., 71
Ethnicity, 9
Europe, 65

Fallon, D., 40, 41
Fayer, J. M., 48
Federico (pseudonymous; ESL learner), 35, 36, 40
Fendler, L., 77
Fermstad, S., 6
Finn-Miller, S., 27–28

Firth, A., 1
Fix, M., 15
Flender, L., 42
Flora (pseudonymous; ESL learner), 36,
    40; dialogue journal of, 37–39
Florez, M. C., 27
Ford, J. K., 70
Freeman, D. E., 58–60
Freeman, Y. S., 58–60
Freire, P., 40, 41
Friends (television program), 26
Frota, S., 28

Gardner, R. C., 27
Gass, S. M., 26, 28
GED, 9
Gelatt, J., 15
Generation 1.5, 21
González, N., 40, 49
Gordon, J., 67
Greek language, 22
Greenberg, E., 8, 18
Grieco, E., 65

Hanesch, S., 59
Harada, V. H., 41
Hauser, R. M., 21
Holistic perspective, 28–29. See also
    Whole-language learning
Holmes, V. L., 36
Holton, E. F., 70
HR Magazine, 67
Huber, W., 36
Huckin, T., 26
Huerta-Macial, A., 16
Human resource managers, 67–69
Hutchins, H. M., 70

Incidental vocabulary learning, 26
Income, 19; distribution of, by prose lit-
    eracy level, 20
Independent learners, 31
Inquiry-based lessons, 29. See also
    Whole-language learning
Institute of Education Sciences (U.S.
    Department of Education), 8
Instrumental motivation, 27
Integrative motivation, 27
Irizarry-Vicenti, M., 46

Jiménez, R. T., 38
Jin, Y., 8
Johnson, K. E., 1
Journal writing, 35–43; assessing, 37; and
    collectively establishing guidelines,
36–37; and guided practice, 37; and
    implementing dialogue journal (DJ),
    36–37; providing model for, 36. See
    also Dialogue Journal (DJ)
Justin (emergent instructor), 25, 31–32

Kamhi-Stein, Lia, 50–51
Keeton, M. T., 71
Kim, J., 42
Koenig, J. A., 21
Kormos, J., 27
Krashen, S. D., 26
Krhahn, M. T., 71
Kubo, H., 15, 20
Kutner, M., 8
Kyambi, S., 65

La familia, 47
Lantolf, J. P., 28
LaPorte, C., 36
Larrotta, C., 3, 35, 36, 75
Larsen-Freeman, D., 66
Latin America, 29
Laufer, B., 26
LEP. See Limited English proficiency
    (LEP)
Limited English proficiency (LEP):
    defining, 7–8; definitions of, in
    reporting NAAL findings, 7–8; and
    Generation 1.5, 21; and types of profi-
    ciency, 7
Literacy skills: assessing, of adult immi-
    grants and adult English language
    learners, 5–23; and defining limited
    English proficiency, 7–8; and prose lit-
    eracy levels of adults, by English lan-
    guage learner status, 2003, 15f
Lladó-Torres, N., 46
López, Y., 46
Luke, C., 28
Lum, D., 41

Macias, R. F., 16, 18
Madsen, R., 2
Marsick, V., 71
Martin, N., 66
Martinez, T. E., 5, 66
Martinsen, R. A., 3, 55, 59, 76
Martinson, K., 15, 20
McCroskey, J. C., 48
McGrath, S., 66
McHugh, M., 15
Miller, E. R., 1
Mohr, Nicholassa, 49
Moll, L., 40, 49

Morales, B., 3, 45; personal account of, 47; personal account of ESL identity of, 49–50
Moreno, K., 59
Morita, N., 61
Moskowitz, G., 51
Motivation, 27
Moulton, M. R., 36

NAAL. *See National Assessment of Adult Literacy* (NAAL; National Center for Educational Statistics)
National Assessment of Adult Literacy (NAAL; National Center for Educational Statistics), 3, 6–23; categories and subcategories of participants in, 8f; data, 8–11; and defining limited English proficiency, 7–8; definitions used in reporting findings of, 7–8
National Center for Educational Statistics (NCES), 3, 6, 8, 10–13, 19
National Center on Immigration Integration Policy, 65–66
National Research Council, 21
NCES. *See* National Center for Educational Statistics (NCES)
New York (state), 6
Nieto, S., 49
Nord, W., 66
Nunan, D., 61

Ohio, 72
Oral proficiency, 18
Oxford, R., 27

Pablo (pseudonymous; ESL learner), 36, 40
Paribakht, T. S., 26
Pasión, 47
Paulsen, C., 8
Peyton, J. K., 26, 35, 36, 42
Pica, T., 28
Populations Division of the Department of Economic and Social Affairs (United Nations Secretariat), 2
Portes, A., 65
Pousada, A. F., 46
Powrie, J., 5
Proficiency: and defining limited English proficiency, 7–8; types of, 7
ProLiteracy Worldwide, 62
Prose literacy level: of adults, by English language learner status, 15f; distribution of household incomes of English language learners by, 20 Fig. 1.3; and employment status, 19 Tab. 1.6; of English language learners, compared with those with below-basic literacy skills, 15–16; English language learners scoring below-basic in, distributed by years living in United States and age of immigration, 16t; and Spanish-speaking status, 23t
Puerto Rican experience: Betsy's personal account of, 47, 49–50; Eileen's personal account of, 47–48, 50–52; ESL teacher identity and classroom practice in, 48; and identity issues in building ESL community, 45–52; and students served, 46
Puerto Rico, 3–4; factors affecting ESL teaching and learning in, 48; language history of, 45–46
Putnam, R. D., 2

Real Women Have Curves (movie), 49
Reed, L., 42
Reese, L., 45
Respeto, 47
Rhodes, D., 18
Richer, E., 15, 20
Richmond, V. P., 48
Rios, A., 50
Rivera, K. M., 16
Russian language, 22

Sagers, S., 36
Santiago, Esmeralda, 49
Scheckley, B. G., 71
Schmidt, R., 28
Schwarzer, D., 3, 25, 28
Second-language acquisition (SLA), research on, 25–28
Seller, D. L., 70
Sergiovanni, T. J., 42, 56, 58, 60
Shearin, J., 27
Snyder, W., 67
Social contracts: on first day, 56–58; in short-term programs, 55–56
Social covenants: on first day, 56–58; in short-term programs, 55–56
Social-change-based language learning, 62–63
Society for Human Resource Managers, 67
Somalia, 72
Soroui, J., 3, 5
South America, 65
Souza, K., 41

Spanish language, 3–4
Staring, R., 65
Staton, J., 36
Stewart, I., 66
Strawn, J., 15, 20
Sullivan, W. M., 2
Sum, A., 5, 6
Swidler, A., 2

Taengnoi, S., 65
Tarone, E., 1
Task-based language learning, 61–62
Teaching English as a second language (TESL), 47, 51
Teaching English to Speakers of Other Languages (TESOL) conference, 50–51
TESL. See Teaching English as a second language (TESL)
Texas, 72
Tipton, S. M., 2
Training and development professionals, 70–71
Tran, Q., 65
Tyler, K., 67, 68

Ullman, C., 52, 75
University of Puerto Rico-Mayaguez (UPRM), 46, 47, 51
UPRM. See University of Puerto Rico-Mayaguez (UPRM)
Uraguay, 47
U.S. Census Bureau, 6
U.S. Department of Education, 10–13, 19; Institute of Education Sciences, 8
Uvin, J., 6

Vélez, J. A., 46
Vocabulary building, 26
Vygotsky, L., 1

Wagner, J., 1
Wang, T., 5, 66
Watkins, K., 71
Wenger, E., 67
Wesche, M. B., 26
White, S., 3, 5, 9
Whole-language learning, 25–32; and acquiring new literacy habits, 31; and alternative assessment, 30; and authentic learning, 29; and capitalizing on learners' expertise, 30–31; and community of learners, 30; and creating independent learners, 31; and curriculum negotiation, 29; and holistic perspective, 28–29; and inquiry-based lessons, 29; and language learning as developmental process, 29; and review of adult second-language acquisition research, 25–28; and teaching whole adult learner, 30–32
Wilcox, B., 36
Wiley, T. G., 5, 16
Wink, J., 41, 42
Wrigley, H. S., 3, 5, 6, 15, 20, 22, 69, 71

Yoon, K., 69, 71

Zarate, M. E., 45
Zuengler, J., 1